Not Right, Not Wrong, Just Different, written by my friend Wallace Mitchell, is a refreshing read. To anyone searching for insights into experiencing health in their relationship with their spouse, this book is for you! I highly recommend this inspiring book to anyone desiring to gain a clear perspective on how a husband and wife can practically learn to really love one another. Thanks, Wallace, for your vulnerability and thanks for this vital contribution to thousands of marriages that will experience a healed and healthy relationship by following the truths found in this book.

—*Larry Kreider, author and International Director of DOVE Christian Fellowship Int'l*

Not Right, Not Wrong
Just Different

Wallace Mitchell III

Partnership
Publications

A Division of House to House Publications

ISBN   978-0-9817765-2-1

Partnership Publications
A Division of House to House Publications
www.H2HP.com

Printed in the United States of America

Dedication

This book is dedicated to my wife, Linda,
and the covenant of marriage.

Acknowledgments

With reverent awe, a deep thanks to the Lord Jesus Christ who called me, saved me, and taught me to trust Him, "being fully persuaded that God had power to do what he had promised" (Rom. 4:21).

To my precious wife Linda, whose insight, gifts and sacrificial giving of herself have been one of God's greatest encouragements in my life. I love her deeply.

To our wonderful children Mitch and Nicole who have always been our joy. They not only lived through our marriage trials, but they used the lessons learned to build their own healthy families.

Thanks to Larry Kreider who gave me an avenue to write this book and thanks to Karen Ruiz and Sarah Sauder who did all the work.

Thanks Pastor Minter who was my first teacher in the Word of God.

Thanks to Pastor Milliken and Mrs. Milliken, who served 30 years as missionaries in the Congo from the 1920's to 1950's. They showed me how to put aside self interests and to set my heart on Jesus. Their words still ring in my ears, "I pray for you every day." I know heaven rejoices because they are now home with the Lord they loved so much, their dear Jesus.

Contents

Not Right, Not Wrong, Just Different

Not Right, Not Wrong, Just Different

Foreword

I knew Wallace and Linda's story before I met them. I knew how their struggles had led to a two-year separation. Their marriage had been all but dead, yet they found a way to restore their relationship and save their family.

I wanted to interview them because I thought their journey would be instructive to other couples facing a marriage crisis. They would be featured in a marriage crisis intervention project I was developing.

What I was not prepared for was how healthy their relationship was. Wallace and Linda graciously invited us to their home and allowed us to videotape an interview with them in which they were totally transparent on the struggles they faced. The amazing thing was there was such dissonance between the crisis they described as I interviewed them and the relationship they live today. During my time with them, they were warm, gracious hosts who were affectionate, loving and respectful of each other. Their bond was, and still is, very deep.

It's obvious that whatever they did to restore their marriage worked! That's why I am excited that Wallace has written this book and so openly shares that story. They lived through a crisis that would destroy most marriages and now are helping other couples build their relationship on a solid foundation while growing daily in love and respect toward each other.

This book is a treasure refined out of personal pain, followed by the insight Wallace and Linda have gained through years of helping and counseling other couples. Your marriage will be better as you follow the concepts Wallace presents in this book.

I enthusiastically recommend it.

Steve Grissom
Founder and President
DivorceCare/Church Initiative
www.churchinitiative.org

Introduction

Linda and I were married December 21, 1968. We have two grown children and four lovely grand-children. I began my career working for the CIA from 1973 to 1989. I left the CIA to become an associate Pastor at Reston Bible Church. After serving there 10 years, Linda and I were sent out to start Broadlands Community Church. We have had the privilege to serve in a variety of ministries which helped give us a broad view of church service. However, the foundation of our approach to ministry came from lessons we learned through our marriage difficulties. God's training through that difficult time has given me and Linda a passion for couples and the insight to minister to them.

Linda and I were high school sweethearts. We dated two years, and then got married at the tender, young ages of 19 and 20. We didn't know much for 19 and 20-year-olds! Linda was a total mystery to me! I didn't understand her and she didn't understand me. After 10 years of misunderstandings, arguments, and frustrations, we separated for two and a half years. During that time we started to learn what it takes to work through our differences and allow them to complement and strengthen our marriage, rather than tear it apart.

Over the years, as Linda and I shared what we learned with others, we witnessed miraculous improvements in people's marriages. We have presented what we learned in a marriage class called the "Relationship Series." Now it is offered in this book. Much of what I share with you in this book came from trying to understand my wife of 40 years. It includes our candid and sometimes rocky story, and it may sound familiar to many. This book does not offer quick solutions, but rather helps give insight to what makes a man and a woman tick and how to work with each other, rather than against each other within the dynamics of marriage. These are the principles Linda and I use in all our couple's counseling. We have consistently seen tremendous improvement in difficult marriage situations.

Although it took me a long time to learn, I discovered that both husbands and wives can de-mystify their differences by recognizing how God designed men and women to be different in order to accomplish His good purposes. Although both men and women have a tremendous responsibility to ensure they have a healthy marriage, *I tend to focus a little more on the husband's need to understand the unique make-up of his wife*. Hopefully, by the end of the book it will become apparent why this was necessary. Join with me in a real life account of two people learning to appreciate and honor their differences.

Wallace Mitchell III
Ashburn, Virginia
May 2009

I Was Mystified

For the first ten years of our marriage I didn't understand Linda. I don't think I understood one thing about her. Our marriage became one long series of arguments that never seemed to end. We would really go at it, fighting verbally and incessantly. I couldn't understand why she couldn't get her act together and she couldn't understand why I just didn't *understand* anything about her. Every day was an absolute shock to me. I kept thinking, *Well, one day she will just get over it and we will be able to have a normal and peaceful life.* But she never got over it, and she remained the biggest mystery in my life!

I tried to understand her. At least, I really thought I was trying, but she would continually surprise me. I would come home from work and be totally unprepared for what she would say, why she would say it, or what she meant! To make matters worse, she would often inform me that she was "the easiest person in the world to understand." That statement never ceased to amaze me. I didn't understand *anything* about her. Not one thing!

It seemed as though we never came to the same conclusions. We would often blame each other for how the other person made *us* feel, without a thought for how our words made *them* feel. I often would say, "What is *wrong* with you?" It took me years to realize that asking my wife that question was not a good approach in the art of communication. We collected a dirty laundry list of negative communication patterns and attitudes.

One day, after ten years of unresolved conflicts, she finally had enough. Basically she said, "I'm done. I'm finished." I was shocked. I did not understand. Why did she want to quit completely? I was trying, and it made me angry that she was ready to quit.

We separated for two and a half years. During the first year of the separation, I went off the deep end. I thought, "Fine, if you think I'm bad, I'll show you bad!" This led to foolish behavior and an immoral relationship.

The Lord wouldn't let me continue to wallow in my wretchedness. After a year of separation, the Holy Spirit convicted me that I needed to do everything I could to repair our failed marriage. Not surprisingly, by this time, our communication was almost at zero. Nevertheless, because of our children, we had periodic contact, and during those times we tried to maintain a civil attitude with each other.

Being convicted to repair the marriage, I finally approached Linda about my intentions. Imagine how that went over! After all those years of a deteriorating marriage, I was already at a double-digit-negative-number in Linda's eyes. Now, in her estimation, my year-long freefall into depravity had positioned me off the charts.

My request to try to repair our marriage elicited a stunned reply of, "You have got to be kidding!"

I was not deterred. I was determined to work on our marriage and to understand what made Linda tick. The task seemed insurmountable because we were so utterly different and viewed life from completely different perspectives.

Even though she was a mystery to me, I knew that God's vision for marriage was oneness, according to Genesis 2:24: "This explains why a man leaves his father and mother and is joined to his wife, and the two are united into one." I also knew that the Bible said that a husband must love his wife just as Christ loved the church and gave up His life for her. I was willing to take God at His word and give it a try.

Subsequently, after the first year of our separation, I started to really pay attention. Since Linda had given up on the marriage, I had to move forward and expect *nothing* in return. I needed to learn to love unconditionally, as Christ loves.

I realized that Linda no longer trusted that I had her best interests in mind. She had emotionally shut down in order to try to protect herself after years of hurt and misunderstandings. I knew I had to do everything I could to try to understand Linda's heart.

Cracking the communication code

I remembered that Linda had always said that she was the simplest person in the world to understand. If that was true, and she had convinced me it was, I thought, *It kind of makes me the dumbest person in the world because I cannot understand anything about her!* Since I didn't want to be the dumbest person in the world, I decided I was going to try to understand how she thinks and why she does things the way she does them.

By the way, after 40 years of marriage, I can now tell you that Linda is one of the most complicated people I have ever known in my life. It is a good thing I didn't know that back then or I might have given up and not tried to understand her at all. The task would have seemed too big. However, I now know why she said that she was the simplest person in the world to understand: *Because she totally understood herself.*

So believing she *is* simple to understand—I would just have to crack the code.

What I did next was so very *male*! I tried to look for consistencies. I wanted to quantify those consistencies so I could understand them. It actually did help. I finally started to understand some things about her. The following pages are filled with examples of that journey.

Another surprising benefit to this journey, I discovered that all couples have three major differences that they bring into marriage that affect it to its very core. They respond to circumstances very differently because of the differences of *culture, personality, and gender.* A failure to recognize and appreciate these differences can become a lifelong source of frustration and disappointment that could lead to the eventual downfall of a relationship.

The differences of culture

When couples come together, they come from two distinct family cultures, or family patterns. Every family has a distinct way of operating and handling family relationships. As we grow up, we learn to operate within that family culture.

Obviously we noticed things about our family and parents that we didn't like. In light of these experiences, we often decide that we will not do what our parents did. Instead, we will change what we perceive as negative family patterns. When we change the things in our family culture that we think are wrong, we believe we change them for the better. We have discovered a better way, and it is now the best way, in our belief.

Consequently, we marry a spouse who has done the same thing concerning their family culture. So now, there are two people who think they are each right in the changes and adjustments they made to improve the state of affairs in their lives.

Two "right" people who have a disagreement do not get very far. Each one believes they cannot be at fault, because they are "right." Each one thinks, "I've already changed the things I needed to change."

Both the husband and wife tend to believe that the unique culture that has been built into them and the memories they cherished or the things they have changed are the correct way of thinking. So, when our spouse has a different take on the matter, we make a judgment. We come to the conclusion that what our spouse thinks is illogical, mistaken, wrong, stubborn, mean, hurtful, insensitive, and the list goes on.

Let me share an example some couples have struggled with. Hopefully, this will help provide insight to understand the multitude of unique cultural differences a marriage may experience. Take, for example, the way a husband and wife think Christmas should be celebrated. When you have two people, both with fond memories of Christmas ever since they were little children, you can easily have tensions that escalate into life-sized problems around Christmas time. One spouse remembers how relatives would come over on Christmas eve, in their best-dressed attire, and lay out a big dinner and then gather around the Christmas tree and sing carols, open up presents and stay late into the night visiting before they went to bed. The other spouse remembers how they woke up very early Christmas day and the excitement of ripping open the presents, lounging around all morning in their pajamas, and playing with their new toys.

Now these two people are married and they have to decide, "When do we open our presents?" "When do we get together with relatives?"

You may say, "Oh, they just have to compromise. It is no big deal."

You want to bet on it? The truth is that both husband and wife have those memories printed indelibly in their minds from childhood. Now, one spouse tells the other that they can't enjoy Christmas the way they remembered it. Instead, they must celebrate Christmas the way *their* family did it.

There is no right or wrong way of doing Christmas, but to each spouse, ingrained in their way of thinking, breaking Christmas traditions can lead to severe family tensions. They may survive the first Christmas, but then it comes around next year and they have to live through it again. They rehash it and they become even more irritated.

Now, this is an example of only one cultural difference. The issue is that there are hundreds of them. Each of them can cause tensions from money management, to sharing household work, to activities with friends, to raising children. We can start to argue about how to hang up our clothes, stack food in the pantry, mow the lawn and discipline the children.

These are issues that can gnaw at us. The reality is that most of the cultural differences are not right or wrong issues. They are *just different.*

The differences of personality

Most people may have taken a personality test. Often workplaces require them before hiring because they are usually quite accurate, telling us how we are wired and how we will react under different types of situations. My intention here is not to identify each person's personality, or even to give a detailed understanding of the differences. My desire is to draw attention to the fact that couples tend to have different personalities and each personality type is good and God given. These different personalities within a marriage should complement one another. A personality test called the DISC includes four main categories of people's behavioral styles: D (dominance) is the driver, doer, task-oriented person; I (influence) is a people-oriented individual who usually doesn't focus on the task. They like to talk and be around people; S (steadiness) is a person who likes small groups. They are sensitive to how people operate, and make a good diplomat; C (conscientiousness) behavioral styles are the detail people. They ask "why" and are good accountants, making sure every "i" is dotted and "t" is crossed.

These four behavioral styles can intermix and it can get much more complicated. No one has a pure, one-dimension behavioral style. Again, the purpose here is not to identify one's behavioral style, but to be aware that there are different behavioral styles and learn to appreciate them.

What is interesting about personality types and marriage is that, very often, opposites attract. I used to wonder, *Why on earth would God create us with such different personalities, making it so difficult to see eye-to-eye in marriage—especially why do opposites attract?*

Here's an example: Emily is a "people person" who loves people and doesn't care if she gets anything done as long as she has people to talk to. She marries Ryan, a detailed guy who likes everything in order and where it's supposed to be. Emily looks at her life which is often in total chaos, and she is drawn to Ryan because he is so perfect and neat. He, in his order and perfection, looks over at this lively girl, full of life and fun. Since he is often bored stiff with his orderly ways, he thinks, *What a refreshing person!* They are both drawn to each other and they are happy—until they say, "I do!"

One day, soon after they are married, Emily walks into the house, throws her coat haphazardly across the couch, and Ryan starts having heart palpitations! A coat is not supposed to be thrown across a couch. It is supposed to be hung up. It is out of order, and something bad is going to happen. He doesn't know what, but it will! The universe is out of sync. He sees nothing but the coat on the couch. "The place is a mess," Ryan says. "Please hang up your coat!"

Emily responds casually, "Pardon me? What mess? What are you talking about? I'll get around to picking it up." And she does, but in her own time, and it is never soon enough for Ryan.

Before long, they want to take a vacation. Emily says, "You know what I would love to do? Let's drive to Florida. Let's just take some money and see where the road leads us."

Again, Ryan's heart starts to race, "No plan? No, no, we *must* have a plan. Give me a map and a highlighter and I will trace a route to Florida, noting the best rest stops, gas stations, places to eat, and Starbucks along the way. I will calculate exactly how much money we will need to go there and back."

Emily's eyes widen in surprise and disappointment. "That's not a vacation! That's a death march! That's no fun. Go by yourself!"

Emily and Ryan's interaction shows us the vast differences in personality we have. These differences really start at conception. When we come into this world, we come with a personality. Granted, we grow and mature, but we are stamped with a unique personality from conception.

When Linda was pregnant with our son, Mitch, he probably kicked in the womb about four times the entire pregnancy. Once born, he was a most content, laid-back baby. Linda would be washing the dishes, and he would sit in his seat and fold his hands and just watch her contentedly. All the previous information we had received about how hard it was to have a new baby in the house didn't apply. *Raising a new baby is a piece of cake*, we thought.

Then five years later, Linda became pregnant with our daughter. One day I came home from work to find Linda moaning on the sofa, and massaging her 8-month pregnant belly. Her belly was pulsating and gyrating up and down and from side to side. It looked like the baby would put her foot through Linda's stomach right then and there! Our daughter came into this world vibrating. From a tiny infant, you could never hold her close. She liked to be held around her waist so she could kick her little hands and feet constantly. Before she learned to walk on her own, she loved her little walker with wheels that gave her the autonomy to sit in the seat, kicking with her feet and start sailing across the hardwood floor. As soon as she would gain speed, she would hold up her little feet and start to spin out of control crashing into the wall. She then would spin around and continue ready for another collision.

As she grew older, she was very athletic. We got her involved in every sport we could because she had so much energy to expend. Not surprisingly, she ended up with a full scholarship playing basketball at North Carolina State University.

Our two children are wired totally different. Now I ask you, "Which personality is the right personality?" Of course there is no right or wrong. They are *just different!* But the truth is that we often irritate each other with our very unique personalities.

When two people marry, they often start to get annoyed by their spouse's personality and see it as irritating or inferior. We are not talking about sin or baggage we bring into a marriage; we are just talking about being alive and the God given differences at play between personalities!

While cultural and personality differences may be the source of misunderstanding and conflict, with deliberate communication and an honest attempt to understand one another, most couples can work through the differences. However, the gender differences may prove to be a much more mystifying problem.

Questions for Reflection
Chapter 1

1. What are some unique family traits that each one of you have brought into your relationship? How have you adjusted to them?

2. What are some personality traits that have tended to clash in your relationship? How have you reconciled them?

Notes

Not Right, Not Wrong, Just Different

Chapter 2

More Than Mystified

The differences of culture and personality for some couples may be varied and extreme. For Linda and me, this was challenging, but the differences of gender almost proved to be too incomprehensible for us to grasp.

The differences of gender

Being separated and attempting to restore our marriage forced me to try and understand the gender differences with greater sensitivity. Again, I was looking for consistencies in behavior, a way to connect the dots. There had to be some logic. As I looked at Linda, I certainly understood that we were different in gender and related behavior. I asked myself, *What are the consistencies in the differences between men and women?* I concluded that women are consistently more sensitive than men. This is not to say that men are not sensitive, but women tend to be more so. Okay, so this wasn't rocket science, but for me it was a big breakthrough.

Moreover, women are usually more relational. What I mean by *relational* is that they speak in more relational ways. **Even when they make a statement of fact, there is a relational message woven into the statement.** As an example, a factual request could be combined with the unspoken relational message of *do you care, am I important, or do you enjoy being with me.* The relational message touches the heart and personal aspects of the factual activity requested. A woman speaks with two messages every time she says something. She doesn't do it on purpose. It is her makeup, because she is more relational and sensitive.

For a case in point, let's say an instructor is teaching a seminar to ten women in a room. The instructor tells them he needs to take a break and will be back in five minutes. When he returns, they are out of their seats, animatedly talking to each other. If the instructor does the same thing to a group of men, he could return in fifteen minutes and they are still in their seats staring at the wall. And they are quite content looking at the wall!

Now focusing on men, I concluded that they are usually driven by goals and facts. They need a goal to function, and once they accomplish that goal, they need another one. They are also interested in facts. "How do I obtain that goal?"

Sometimes even marriage itself can be treated as a *goal* by a man. Once he has reached the goal of marriage, he moves on to the next goal. He has the sense of satisfaction from an accomplishment. Resting in that accomplishment, he may not realize the continuous nature of keeping the relational fires burning. It is not that he doesn't appreciate his marriage or wife, but flowers, candy, and dating may not be seen as necessary any longer. It is like deer hunting. He shoots and bags the deer, puts the antlers over the mantle and goes on to other things because the goal is achieved.

With these natural gender differences, communication can become almost impossible. When a wife says to her husband, "Let's just talk," a husband thinks *Talk? About what?* (Warning: The relationship starts to nose-dive quickly with that particular response!) But the truth is, if a man doesn't have a goal to fulfill, it seems pointless to him to "just talk."

Often in a disagreement with his wife, a husband will say, "What do you want me *to do?*" He is saying, "What is the goal? What are the facts necessary to achieve the goal?" What he really means is, "What can I do to *end* this?" He wants his "talking" to ensure a definite end to the disagreement. His world is filled with facts and goals and resolutions! Once the goal is achieved it is not necessary to continue the discussion.

In contrast, if a wife feels she and her husband are not communicating, she says to her husband, "We aren't talking." She means, "We need to relate, share our feelings, and have quality time together."

Her husband may be clueless to what she really means and may respond, "Sure we did; yesterday at 4:00 p.m., we talked." These types of comments can keep him in "hot water" and he may never know why.

Again, it is worth repeating, husbands, you must learn that your wife communicates two messages every time she says something. There is the factual message and there is the relational message.

Here is an example of this scenario between a husband and wife: The husband comes home for dinner. They both have worked all day, and the wife suggests they go out for dinner.

He says, "No, I don't want to go out. I have had a difficult day."

She says, "Fine."

But the husband sees that she seems a little irritated. In a marriage, a "one word" answer from one's wife is rarely a sign of being okay. So the husband takes the time to explain why he doesn't want to go. On a factual level, he explains why he's too tired and why it is a bad idea.

Now she's even more upset than before. Why? Because when a woman speaks, she is not only stating facts, she is also stating something relational. *Would you take me out to dinner?* is the fact, but here the underlying relational message is, *Do you love me enough to take me out to dinner?* To a wife, she may be asking how she rates in her husband's life.

News flash!

When the relational message is, *Do you love me enough to take me out to dinner?* The correct answer is never just a factual, "No!" The husband will say, "I didn't say that!" In this case, the husband has to realize that when he simply answered with facts, he has ignored her relationally. In worse case scenarios, he may have communicated to his wife that he does not love her enough or care about her enough to take her out to dinner. At this point, he has dug himself into a hole, and now she may not even go out with him anyway!

When a wife asks a question, a husband must make an effort to answer the relational question, first, not the factual one. Once he answers the relational question, the factual question usually is not such a source of misunderstanding, tension, or conflict. To her question, "Will you take me out to dinner?" he can answer, "Honey, you are the most precious person in the world to me and I would love to take you out, but I had a difficult day at work." Because he has made a connection with her relationally, he has communicated that she is important to him. She now knows that he cares about how she feels and she will more than likely accept the fact that he would rather not go out that particular evening.

Another example of this would be when a wife asks her husband to do some chores around the house. She says to him, "Would you fix the faucet *for me*?" The husband gives a detailed explanation about why he can't fix it now—he has five other projects that need attention first. After they are accomplished, then he will get to it. He immediately sees that she is not happy!

If he can rewind the conversation, he will realize that he forgot to look at the relational part of that request. It dawns on him that the important part of her request was *for me*. She is subconsciously wondering how she rates in his life. She asked him to fix something, and he responded that she rated about number six in his life, because he had five other things that were more important than what she requested.

Of course, she is probably not thinking this overtly; it is just built into her way of thinking because she is sensitive and relational. If a husband succeeds in explaining thoroughly the importance of all of his other tasks, he thoroughly convinces her she is number six, and she will *feel* like number six! That's why a husband can stay in trouble—his logic is good, but he is not answering the relational questions his wife is asking.

Husbands, if you are wondering what the correct answer to the faucet-fixing question is, try this: "I love you more than anything in the world, and I want to fix the faucet because you are special to me, but I have a couple of things to get finished today. Would tomorrow be okay?" This response answers the wife's relational question and allows the discussion to proceed on a factual level.

If a husband thinks, "Why can't she just say what she means, and mean what she says?" He is asking her to just state the facts and forget about being sensitive and the relational characteristics that make up who she is. He is asking her to stop being *female*. We will talk more about this later.

Not right or wrong—*just different!*

Listen up, husbands. This is an important key to understand. These styles of communication are not a matter of being right or being wrong. They are **just different**.

As soon as a husband or a wife says the other is wrong, they are doing nothing to understand where the other spouse is coming from because they are now thinking in terms of right and wrong. However, if both the husband and wife see it as simply *different*, they may try harder to understand what is going on with their spouse and endeavor to make adjustments.

"Understanding that differences are not intentional…can make a huge difference in a relationship," states psychologist Michael G. Conner. "The differences that can be sensed between a man and woman can deepen their relationship. More importantly, when men seek to understand and appreciate that which is feminine, they come to a deeper understanding of their self. And when a woman seeks to understand that which is masculine in men, they come to appreciate and understand more about their self." [1]

When husbands and wives learn to accept their differences and make adjustments, they avoid perceiving their differences as personal attempts to frustrate each other.[2]

In other words, a husband does not have to become more sensitive and relational like a woman, but instead can approach the situation so that he allows *her* to be who God created *her* to be—sensitive and relational. In this way, he is seeking to understand those underlying relational questions his wife is asking and answer her questions based on their love relationship.

If he allows her to be sensitive, she will be sensitive to those things around her, including her husband. However, if a husband keeps ignoring the relational and sensitive aspect of his marital relationship, his wife may turn the sensitivity and relational part off, and she will no longer be sensitive to her husband.

Likewise, wives can be their sensitive, relational selves and yet communicate facts that their husbands need to help them in a conversation. She needs to attempt to articulate in a way that gives him an avenue to understand her heart. Sometimes a statement like, "I need you to listen to me, but I don't need you to fix anything," can alert the husband to tune in relationally.

What's on your love pile?

It is futile to try to change a spouse's family culture, or personality, or the way they operate in their gender. By trying to do so, husbands or wives are in effect destroying the other person by telling them that they are wrong.

When you tell someone they are wrong, you send them three messages: "There is something about you I don't like!" "I don't like you!" and "I don't love you!"

Often in marriage, the "you are wrong" messages are similar to little, tiny straws that pile up over the years to become an enormous pile. Like one piece of straw after another piled on top of a camel, one day the last straw is added to the pile and it causes the camel to collapse. At the camel's collapse couples often (desperately) go to marriage counseling. They attempt to pull out different straws and try to decide which one broke their marriage. I can assure you, it wasn't just one straw——it was the accumulation of the large pile!

Conversely, the "I love you" messages tend to pile on in a very different way. *I love you enough to take you out to dinner. I love you enough to fix the faucet. I want to protect your sensitivity.* All these constant and reassuring messages that say, "I love you," pile on over the years, and without realizing it, you have grown a dynamic marriage! People may ask you, "What did you do to have such a great marriage?" You may not be sure exactly what it was that you did, except to pile on all those little messages that said, "I love you," which added up to something phenomenal!

When couples come to me for marriage counseling, they usually have a dire issue they are trying to come to grips with. They believe that a certain situation is destroying their marriage, and, I may agree that it is bad. However, what I often realize is that the situation we are talking about is not the exact circumstance destroying their marriage. It is just evidence of a history of "I don't love you" messages that have culminated in their current state of affairs. The "I don't love you" messages over the years have finally exploded into this one dire situation. Now they are trying to fix the problem, but they can't because it is built on so many accumulated issues.

Not Right, Not Wrong, Just Different

To fix a marriage, you have to start pulling out the straws, one at a time, that say, "I don't love you," and replace them with the ones that say instead, "I love you!"

After ten years of marriage, Linda finally shut down emotionally toward me. Somewhere along the way that final straw was added; that final "I don't love you" was communicated. Because I did not understand the messages that I was sending, I did not understand her behavior. Therefore, I reacted by saying, "What is wrong with you?"

For years Linda would respond, "You are chipping away at my heart." When I write that now, it sends chills down my spine. When she told me I was chipping away at her heart, I could not comprehend what she was talking about. I did not understand it then, but now I know exactly what I did to her. I had not heard her relational messages to me. I had ignored them for years.

The night that the final straw broke the camel's back, all she could manage was, "I'm sorry. I'm sorry, but I don't love you anymore." As a sensitive and relational female, she was sorry for how she felt, but she could not get out from under all the straw that had piled on and weighed her down to the breaking point.

I remember thinking, "What do you mean, you are sorry you don't love me? If you are sorry for something, you don't do it." I thought Linda was callously hurting me for no apparent reason, and my gut reaction was, *okay I'll show you!*

And with that attitude, our marriage exploded.

Questions for Reflection
Chapter 2

1. Facts and goals/sensitive and relational, what are some consistent gender differences in your relationship?

2. How does understanding that there is a "relational message" help your communication as a couple?

Notes

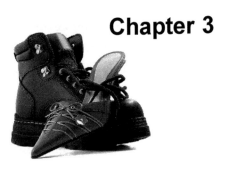

Chapter 3

The Lights Go On!

I was 20 years old, and Linda was 19 when we married. We were not very mature for 19 and 20-year-olds, but we got married anyway! I worked my way through college and Linda also worked to help support us. In one way, it helped to be so busy because we didn't have that much time to spend talking to each other. As the years went by and we had more interaction with each other, more and more difficulties arose. We were so different. We had tremendous difficulty connecting in every way.

I had no clue where she was coming from, and she didn't have a clue where I was coming from. But I held on to the notion that she would just get over it. Well, she never got over it, and this led to our separation of two and a half years.

Finally, after being separated for a year, the futility of going my own selfish way caught up with me. I felt empty inside. The worldly pleasures looked so shallow and meaningless. In the depth of my heart, I believed that God desired for us to have a healthy, loving marriage. For this to happen, I knew that I needed to pay special attention to Linda to

Not Right, Not Wrong, Just Different

discover what made her tick. Unfortunately, I had spent a year "behaving badly" which put me in an even worse position with Linda. After spending the next year and a half totally dedicating myself to understanding her and to being the best husband I could be in a seemingly impossible situation, Linda agreed that we should try to put the family back together. However, she was forthright. She said, "I don't love you, and I don't want to be with you, but I think God wants to put the family back together so you can come back." It was an offer I took her up on, but it was rocky going. After over two years, we were now in the same house together again.

Once we were back together, I made it a point to try to listen to everything she said. Although, on the flip side of the coin, I was scared not to! I really wanted *us* to work.

I remember the first several nights back in the house. She would make dinner for herself and our two young children and set three plates on the table. They ate and she cleaned up the dishes. After they finished, I would go into the kitchen and prepare something for myself to eat. It was tense! The first six months of living together again seemed worse than what we experienced leading up to our separation or even the separation itself.

Linda and I had not been attending church together, but when we got back together she agreed that we should attend as a family. That first Sunday, people would say, "Praise the Lord, Linda and Wallace are together again." I thought to myself, *If you only knew how bad it is, you wouldn't be praising Jesus!*

Nevertheless, I was sincerely trying to understand and figure out how to make the marriage work. I just had no clue how the dots were connected, or the reasons behind why she did anything. In fact, every time she said something, I almost went into a panic, not knowing how to respond because up to this point my responses were usually wrong! Then Linda would become upset, and the cycle would continue again.

As much as I tried, I couldn't figure her out. I literally was trying to respond to every situation by rote memory. For every situation that presented itself, I would try to remember the good answers that triggered good responses from her. Likewise, I would make special note of those answers that would trigger bad responses. However, the mind can only remember so much. To make matters worse, whole new scenarios continually popped up and I had nothing to stand on! I would make a guess and watch the response and then add it to my list. Needless to say, this was a fairly miserable time, but one day, *"The Lights Came On!"*

Shoes on the floor

This following event proved to be one of the most profound in my married life. It may seem insignificant to others, but for me it opened the door to logic, cause and effect, and connecting the dots in my marriage relationship with Linda. In fact, it opened the door for me to understand other marriage relationships. It enabled Linda and me to have a ministry to marriages that has proven fruitful to the present time. This event took place about six months after we had gotten back together and things were still very tense. We lived in a little apartment, and I came home one day and everything was clean and in its place. It was always important to Linda to have the house in order. I thought it was nice that Linda kept it clean, but I grew up in a household where it didn't matter where you threw your coat or kicked off your shoes. My mother, bless her heart, just didn't care if it got messy.

Linda's view of tidy and clean and my view were definitely not the same. Many times when I viewed something as *clean* she thought it was really a *mess*. This particular day I came home, took off my shoes by the door and walked into the living room to watch TV. Our apartment as usual, was spotless. She came into the room, saw my shoes by the door, and said, "Would you take your shoes to the bedroom?"

I said, "Sure."

Now, I didn't do it immediately because I had in my mind that I would do it when I was ready to go to the bedroom later that night. After a while she came through the room again and said, "Would you take your shoes to the bedroom?"

Again, I said, "Yes." But I didn't make a move to do it.

The third time she came into the room, I knew I was in trouble. She was literally shaking with anger. Her face was red and her fists clenched. "Will you take your shoes back to the bedroom?"

I quickly said, "Yes." I immediately picked up the shoes and took them back to the bedroom. At that moment, I felt the safest place to be was in the bedroom. Now, this was not anything unusual. This was just the run of the mill way we lived our lives. But this time, as I stood in our bedroom, I started to think seriously about what had just transpired. Why would anyone get so upset about a pair of *shoes on the floor?*

It was a mystery to me, and I really wanted to understand what had just taken place. I wanted to know *what Linda felt and thought about that pair of shoes on the floor*. I knew I needed to approach her in a way that would not rekindle the conflict.

I got my thoughts together and returned to the kitchen where Linda was preparing dinner. You probably are getting the picture of our life together. We had a history of over a decade together, but today I deeply wanted to know what was going on inside her. Also, this is living proof that a person can stay clueless for a very long time! There is no guarantee that if you stay together, you will understand each other any better!

I entered the kitchen where Linda was working and said in my most diplomatic voice, "I know those shoes on the floor really upset you, and it bothered you that I didn't take those shoes back to the bedroom right away, and I know I should have, but I would just like to know why that upset you so much?" I waited.
She said simply, "If you loved me, you would have taken them back when I asked you the first time."

To be perfectly honest, I thought my head was going to explode. My mind was already boggled, but now my head started to overheat. I struggled to follow her train of thought. *What in the world does picking up a pair of shoes and moving them to another place have anything to do with our love? There is no connection between those shoes and loving Linda. What in the world was she talking about?*

My epiphany

As I stood there trying to grapple with this concept, unexpectedly a light switch flipped on in my head. Now, I am sure it was the hand of God! I suddenly saw the cause and effect of what had just happened. It was important to Linda to have things neat and orderly in our home. This reflected her efforts and her as a person. I would walk in and sabotage what she thought was important by dropping my shoes on the floor. As a result, I was communicating to her that I didn't value her efforts which also communicated I didn't value her as a person. Even worse, to her it meant that I didn't love her. Remember what she said, "If you loved me, you would have taken them back when I asked you."

If this is put into a work situation, it would be like spending hours preparing a report for your boss. When you hand it to him and ask him what he thinks about it, he pours a cup of coffee on it! There is a direct message in that action! *What you did is not important to me!*

Linda would pour herself into making our home clean and orderly and I would come in and drop my shoes, communicating that I didn't care about what she did. Meaning, that I not only did not value what she did, but I did not value her. It was a direct "I don't love you" message to Linda.

Now, this was not a great big "I don't love you" message. It was a little, bitty "I don't love you" message that I had communicated over and over again for 15 years. The communication of small "I don't love you" messages over multiple years are very destructive to a marriage.

I finally realized that, in our house, when I picked up my shoes, hung up my coat or made the bed, it communicated "I love you" to Linda. She received it as *love*. From that moment, I never looked at my shoes on the floor or a coat over a chair the same way.

At last, I understood how I had communicated "I don't love you" messages to Linda over the years. I began to see the relational messages she was communicating and the relational messages I was communicating.

It was clearly noticeable that my life literally changed after that epiphany. I could approach Linda in an understanding way. No more misery of relying on rote memory. I now could see a cause and effect in our relationship. Everything was beginning to make perfect sense.

Rest assured, today I do not give an "I don't love you" message to Linda with my shoes thrown on the floor or a coat flung over a chair. Even more importantly, I learned the secret to giving "I love you" messages. It can be as simple as picking up your shoes off the floor!

What is your "shoes on the floor" situation?

We do not all have the same issues with shoes-on-the-floor or coats-flung-over-chairs." Based on your makeup, you are certain to have your own shoes-on-the-floor situation. If you are arguing about one insignificant thing after another and don't know why, please don't let them pile up. There are many relational causes and effects every couple needs to recognize and discuss. Little arguments pile up and become destructive over the years.

Sometimes it seems so trivial, and it's hard to understand what the underlying issues are. If you want to have a dynamic marriage, you have to figure out your own shoes-on-the-floor issues, identify them, communicate them to one another, and then make adjustments so you can relay "I love you" messages.

By the way, I still am not a tidy person. You wouldn't know it in day-to-day living in our house because I make an effort to pick up and give Linda those "I love you messages"; it almost seems to come as second nature now. If she ever goes away to visit her mother for a week, I don't clean up a thing. I don't make the bed or hang up my clothes. And I always tell Linda, "Don't ever come home early!" The day

Not Right, Not Wrong, Just Different   *41*

before she comes back, I do a thorough house cleaning so that everything is spotless when she arrives home.

It is important to me to tell Linda that I love her. I have made adjustments to communicate that love. Husbands and wives must learn how the dots are connected. They must examine their irritations and discover what is underneath them and learn how to make changes in their subtle messages to each other in order to effectively communicate their love for each other.

Our differences in personality

One day, some years later after the light bulb epiphany of communicating little "I love you" messages, I was in the kitchen straightening it up. I had just spent thirty minutes showing Linda how much I loved her by putting things back in their place. Linda walked by the kitchen door, threw a quick glance into the room and casually said, "Would you pick that up over there?"

Now, I had just finished cleaning the whole kitchen, or so I thought. Her casual comment really upset me. *How could she, in one millisecond, see the one thing I didn't do?* Nevertheless, I bit my tongue and picked up the one thing that I had missed.

I walked down to my basement study, still irritated, but trying to understand how on earth Linda could, in a one millisecond glance, see the one thing I didn't do?

I went back upstairs, walked into the kitchen where Linda was now sitting at the table drinking a cup of tea by the window. To this day, I don't know why I said this, but now I know God must have prompted me.

I walked up to her and said, "I'd like you to do something for me."

"Sure, what?" she said. She had no idea that I had been fuming.

"I want you to glance out the window and then look back at me."

She glanced out the window and looked back at me.

"What did you just see out there?" I asked.

"Well, I saw our dogwood tree. The sun is shining down on the tree, and where the sun is hitting, the leaves look kind of yellow, but where it's shaded, it shows a real dark green color. The blossoms are coming out and each has four petals, and they're a beautiful pink with a dark pink edge. The centers are greenish-yellow with stamens sticking out of them. And the car is parked out front, and it needs to be washed."

Not only was I stunned by the detail, but also by the instantaneous comprehension of all that information. Again, I suddenly realized how different Linda was from me in her personality.

Just then, our fifteen-year-old son walked into the kitchen.

"Son," I said, "I want you to do something; I want you to look out the window."

"Why?" he asked.

"Just look out," I repeated.

Why do you want me to look out the window?" he asked again.

"Just look out the window," I said more sternly. "Take a long look."

After a long look, I told him to turn around and tell me what he saw.

"A tree," he said.

Not Right, Not Wrong, Just Different   43

"Yes, but can you tell me anything else?"

"It's just a tree, dad. Nothing but a tree out there!" he grumbled.

"There's more out there than a tree," I said. "What else?"

He said, "Grass! There's grass!"

Suddenly another light bulb went off in my head. I realized that I walk around in this world and, like my son, see trees and some grass. Linda sees the intricate detail of a tree. She sees individual leaves, petals and also the colors and hues represented.

I realized right then and there that herein lay another huge difference between us. This time it was not a gender difference—it was a difference in personality. Men have this same ability. It reminds me of Ted Williams, a baseball player and one of the greatest hitters of all time. He said he could watch the rotation of the stitching on the baseball as it sped toward him and could predict its final position over the plate four out of every ten times he was at bat.[1] Now that is seeing the details!

Linda is like that. She is extremely observant and sees the details. I thought to myself, *If I saw all that detail at one time, I couldn't stand it. I would scream and cover my eyes!*

You see, my world is much more laid back. I step outside and I see a random tree here and grass there. I can be walking along and things are falling apart and I barely notice them. I'm happy!

When I recognized this difference, I realized it was a big issue in our lives. So many times, I felt like I could not quite get it right for Linda. There was always something else to be done. She saw the details, but they were not as evident or as important to me. To make matters worse, I would often just

Not Right, Not Wrong, Just Different

make the mistake of saying, "Who cares? It's not that important." All these would ultimately come across as more "I don't love you" messages.

I finally realized that seeing the details was not an irritation; *it was a resource*. She sees what I do not. Today, when we go someplace, I always ask her, "What did you see?" I listen to her answer because I know she saw more than I saw! I must say that I have greatly improved in how I see things. By appreciating Linda's gifting, I have learned from her to see more details. Through her example, I have become much more observant.

I still know my limitations. One time we were wallpapering a room and Linda needed a trim border that matched the rest of the room. She showed me a flower in the paper and asked me to go to the store and pick up the paper that matched it. She thought it was an easy task, but I flatly refused. I knew that I would walk into the store and all the flowers would look the same. I just do not see details. I definitely do not see the stitching on the baseball flying by; I barely see the baseball!

Linda is also a lot more intuitive than me. She can meet someone and say to me, "They are not doing too well. I think something is wrong."

"What do you mean?" I say, "They just said *hello!*"

The truth is that Linda picks up on people's countenances and demeanors and how they carry themselves. In light of that intuition,[2] she can often discern if something is going on in their lives.

Make a heart connection

The differences between a man and woman are complex and varied. I am still learning and do not pretend to have all the answers. I do know that with healthy communication a couple will gain a deeper understanding and appreciation for each other.

Communication is the key. Ultimately this builds a healthy relationship and a marriage God always intended. When a couple does not understand these differences of personality in a marriage, it can cause tremendous pain. When I understood the differences between us, I could see logic in our relationship and things became much simpler. I realized that although some wives like chocolates and others like flowers, Linda liked me to pick up my clothes! It was as simple as that. And how hard is that? I learned that it was quite possible for me to give that kind of "I love you" message! I made the choice to always endeavor to make a heart connection rather than argue.

Being observant of emotions helps us to make that heart connection. Emotions often communicate what is going on and can be red flags so we can pay attention to what's really happening in our marriage. One morning I left for work and all seemed well with Linda and me. I called her once or twice during the day and we had a pleasant conversation. That evening, I came home and casually said, "How are you doing?"

She said, "Fine." The single word answer without any additional comments made me suspicious.

"Are you sure?" I asked.

She responded again, "I am fine."

I was fairly certain that she was not fine. In an effort to be sensitive and understand I said, "I know something is bothering you and I want to be a part of what you are feeling. Would you let me?"

"I don't feel like you are taking care of me," she responded.

Wait a minute. Everything had seemed all right this morning, how could things have gone wrong during the eight hours I was at work? I thought.

I said, "Tell me more. How am I not taking care of you? Give me something to hold onto."

"You didn't empty the trash. You didn't sweep off the porch." she said.

"Oh, you're right. I will do them right away," I responded.

"No, it's all right. Don't bother," she said.

I knew this was something I definitely needed to do. So while I was sweeping off the porch, I thought, *Why does having a clean or dirty porch have anything to do with not taking care of her?*

And the answer was clear. When Linda asked me earlier to empty the trash and sweep the porch, and I didn't do them, the message I communicated to her was that I was not taking care of her. Let me restate that. It made her *feel* like I was not taking care of her. I may be splitting hairs but this message is a little different from the "I don't love you" message. However, it does help to know exactly what a person is feeling and why they feel that way. Then conversations can become so much more enlightened.

As a man, I can easily shut the door on the trash that needs to be emptied and forget all about it. But there's something within Linda that causes some "unempted trash tentacles" to run out on the floor, up her leg and into her heart! Therefore, she feels not cared for and ignored.

Since the unemptied trash has that heart connection, I must empty the trash. For us, emptying the trash is relational. It communicates that I am taking care of her.

Work to make healthy connections

Marriage is the height of relationships—the most intense there is. The woman has greater relationship capacity and sensitivity than the man—she is a relational being. Consequently, in the marriage relationship she will express that sensitivity, and the husband needs to pay attention. She has capacities he does not have. If a husband does not make an attempt to hear what his wife says and become in tune with her feelings, he may think what she says *must* be wrong or something is wrong with her, because often the "relationship" stuff just doesn't make sense to him!

Remember, guys usually communicate *facts* and women communicate *relationally*.

A message to wives: Please do not think, "Well, my husband ought to know what to do. If I have to tell him, then it is not worth it." The truth is—he does not know! You must articulate what you feel so a husband can understand what is going on inside.

A message to husbands: Be aware that something is going on inside her so that you can receive it when she expresses it. When she articulates it, then you can hear her heart and make an effort to understand. In doing so, you can make that healthy connection!

Questions for Reflection
Chapter 3

1. What are your "shoes on the floor"?

2. As a couple what has been a "dogwood tree" experience for you?

Notes

Not Right, Not Wrong, Just Different

Chapter 4

Work Together in Spite of Differences

"You Complete Me."

If that line sounds familiar it's because I borrowed it from the movie *Jerry Maguire*. It's a story about finding that special someone who brings out the best in you because they fill in all the gaps that you are missing. There is a real truth to that line in a relationship between a man and a woman.

When a husband and wife discover they are not defective just because they are so different, they can move ahead to work together in their uniqueness, complement each other and even enjoy their differences. This knowledge in a marriage relationship is powerful. But how can this connection and interaction happen fluidly? I am going to use an analogy of a battleship and radar to communicate how a man and woman are capable of working together and filling in the gaps the other is missing. Hopefully, this analogy will be beneficial for both the husband and wife to help understand how the other one thinks.

Picture with me a battleship sailing off to fight a battle: The battleship is the man with a mission and task, and the radar atop the battleship is the woman being sensitive and aware of what is around her as the ship moves forward. Let's say the heavily armored battleship is assigned to provide anti-aircraft screening from enemy raids. As it plows ahead, the radar on top is picking up everything coming over the horizon.

Working cooperatively, the radar is functioning to protect the battleship. The battleship must have a focus and be heading in the right direction, but it is the radar that picks up the incoming danger—enemy planes within radar range but as yet unseen to the natural eye. In this way, the battleship will have time to maneuver or fully arm itself before the planes arrive. That's how I see a husband-wife relationship. A woman typically picks up on relational problems before the guy does, and she tries to communicate those to him.

The captain on the battleship is looking to the sky and may see nothing but blue sky, but the radar keeps feeding information that planes are incoming. "Planes, planes, planes!" it warns. The radar has an extremely important function because without the warning the battleship may not realize there is imminent danger.

The danger of turning it off or turning it down!

But what if, with the radar static and noise coming in, the captain says, "This is too distracting and noisy, let's just turn it off so we can concentrate on our mission and target ahead." How foolish is that, in a military sense?

It is just as foolish in a relational sense when a husband says to the wife (radar), "I do not see the problem. There is no need to talk about this anymore. Turn it off." At that, the wife may indeed stop talking. And the husband may think, "Ah, peace!" But that is not peace; it is foolishness. A husband may experience less noise, but it is a false sense of peace. When a husband attempts to turn off the switch to a woman's radar that is picking up sensitive matter, that sensitivity is turned off to her husband as well. Now it may be quiet in the house, but we are headed for destruction in the relationship!

Another mistake a husband can make is to allow the radar to buzz in the background, but make light of what the wife is hearing. He will flippantly respond to his wife's warning messages by saying, "That's dumb" or "You're overreacting!" He hears the chatter, but all he sees is blue sky. He feels like there is way too much noise, and turns down the sensitivity of the radar. Not smart! Now the wife's sensitivity is turned down on everything in their marriage and it even damages the radar. Like a radar screen that becomes damaged and doesn't pick up as much, so the woman becomes damaged by a husband's comments, and subsequently doesn't hear as clearly as she used to. She becomes less sensitive to everything, including her husband.

Now we are in trouble! Planes are coming in, the radar is damaged and there is no warning. Usually it's the husband who is the most surprised. He thinks, "Look at all these problems we are having. I had no idea we were in so much trouble!"

The truth is, when the husband sees the enemy planes, it's usually too late—they are upon him. You may as well begin to count the bombs falling down on top of him. If the husband calls me to initiate marriage counseling, I often think, *Uh oh—ship sunk! This guy is dead in the water; he just doesn't know it yet!* Usually the bow of his marriage is up in the air, the stern is already underwater and going down fast. Now, we are working with a sinking ship, and recovery is harder to manage.

On the other hand, when the wife sees the planes, there is still time, because the radar range is long; she is looking beyond the horizon. When she calls for marriage counseling, there is usually something more to work on. She is hearing the planes coming across the horizon and it is not too late to "man the ship."

How the ship and the radar work seamlessly together

In a marriage relationship, we endeavor to understand each other's makeup so that we can complement each other. This involves working through the differences to make the relationship better. A conscientious captain will take care of the radar on his ship. It needs protection. A husband wants his wife to remain sensitive so she can do her job and pick up incoming signals without interference. As he takes care of his wife, she can do what she does best—be sensitive and relational.

Another interesting thing about radar is that it is so sensitive; it picks up everything—including birds or insects in the area. So, imagine this—the captain is hearing all of the static in one long cacophony—planes, birds, insects, planes, birds, insects!

The tendency of the husband is to say to his wife, "I keep hearing you say, "Planes, planes, planes, but those noises are just birds chirping. What's the big deal?"

To the wife, she is communicating activity on the radar. Her job is to pick up their signals, not to differentiate between them. She brings the signals in, and it is her husband's task to help decipher it.

If the ship and radar are working perfectly, the wife pulls in the signals, and if the husband listens and discusses the different sounds with her and acknowledges the various planes, birds and insects, he can say, "Wow, so you saw that? That is incredible. It was just a bird, and it's not going to bother us, but it's great you are sensitive enough to see it."

Now, the wife knows it's okay to be sensitive and funnel the information to her husband because he will acknowledge it, big or small, and help her to understand it. She now knows that she can tell her husband anything. And he is happy to know that she is so perceptive. The result is that communication increases.

For example, when a wife sees the warning signals in a situation concerning their finances, she may go to her husband and say, "You know our finances are really bad. I think we are going to lose the house. I think we are going to lose the car. In fact, we may even lose the kids!"

Her husband says, "Well, you're right, the money situation is bad. I appreciate you telling me, and it's incredible that you can see that, but I think we can keep the house, the car *and* the kids. It's not going to fall completely apart; it's only a "bird" money situation, and I think we can handle it." In this way, a husband validates what his wife saw, and she will realize she can communicate with him without ridicule for being too cautious. Feeling safe, she will continue to be sensitive and say what she sees more and more often.

This is called a *relationship!* It's communication in a relationship, and every relationship must have good communication.

It's not a science; it's an art

Women are emotional and sensitive beings…on average, more so than men. So when a wife sees things in the marriage relationship that need work, and she brings them up, it is so she can talk about them. Sometimes she may want a resolution or sometimes she may just want to vent. It is important for a husband to listen at these times and to try to ask probing questions, "How would you feel if…?" or "How do you feel when….?" This lowers the feeling of vulnerability for the wife and eases communication.

Even though these interactions may seem frustrating at the time, the exchanges are building relationship and communication—and there is healthy growth in the relationship through this type of open discussion. Husbands, you must step up and protect your wife's sensitivity. She must feel like she can express herself to you anytime and about anything. The more you validate her sensitivities, the safer she feels and the more she communicates with you.

Build relationship and communication

I've said it before and I'll probably repeat it again: We must remember that the way we are made and how we function is not right or wrong; it's **just different!** Because our spouse is so different, we often make wrong assumptions or communicate that he or she is wrong. When that happens, a spouse will start to withdraw, and the communication will break down. Even though a husband may not have a clue where his wife is coming from or why something is such a big deal to her when it hardly matters to him, he is wise to engage and talk to his wife about it. This builds relationship!

When we understand how we are made, we can approach times of conflict with wisdom. A man needs to realize that when he is having a discussion with his wife, it is not like he is discussing something with another guy. To illustrate, let's say we have two objects—a pencil and a flower. If a pencil (representing a man) and a flower (representing a woman) are pressed down firmly onto a flat surface repeatedly and under the exact same amount of pressure, the pencil remains unscathed and rigid, but the flower bends, its petals crumple and even fall off. This is often what happens when a husband and wife come into conflict. They have had a disagreement with equal intensity on both sides. The wife can be emotionally damaged by the discussion or conflict, but the husband doesn't think it's a big deal. As a result, a lot of husbands walk away, winning the battle but ultimately losing the war.

In marriage counseling, when I ask a husband to be aware of the "radar and the flower," I am asking him to adjust his thinking. I am not asking him to be less of a man. Guys just need to adjust their thinking. For instance, they must realize that the ladies are sensitive and most of their communication includes a relational message. Most men can approach something, evaluate it and adjust their approach.

However, in marriage counseling I can't ask the wife to be less sensitive and less relational because I would really be asking her to stop being *female*! I am sure the man really doesn't want his wife to stop being female; therefore, I ask a man to adjust his thinking. He can do that without becoming damaged and still be as masculine as he ever was.

Certainly a wife has a responsibility to understand her husband. She needs to remember that he needs facts and goals and is often confused by or misses the relational message. She needs to attempt to articulate her feelings in such a way that he has something to *grab hold of.* Sometimes with a little understanding, it is not as hard as she may think. When Linda feels full emotionally about a certain situation she will say, "I need to talk to you and I don't need you to fix it!" I breathe a sigh of relief. I know the only goal I have is to listen. Therefore, by listening intently, this problem will go away after we talk with no other action needed on my part.

A case illustrating these points happened when a lady came to see me several years ago for marriage counseling.

"What seems to be the problem?" I asked.

She replied, "I'm crazy!"

"So you really think you're crazy?" I asked.

"Oh yes, I'm crazy," she repeated. I have a wonderful husband, he has a wonderful job, we have a beautiful home, two new cars, three lovely children, and I'm not happy. So I must be crazy."

I asked what her husband thought. She told me that she had talked to her husband many times about her unhappiness, but was unable to explain why she felt the way she did. He thought she was unreasonable and that nothing would make her happy. He, being a man, had focused on the task and did what most men tend to do. He worked harder; he put in more hours at the office and bought her more things, hoping to make her happy.

As I counseled both of them, it became clear that she did not care so much about the house or the cars; she just wanted a close relationship with her husband. In trying to fix the problem, the more he worked to provide her with things to make her happy. By putting more time into his job, he was doing the very things that took away from what she needed: His time!

The more he worked the more she was feeling empty and alone. Through counseling, they realized what the problem was, and he was able to make adjustments in his thinking and his life-style so he could spend more quality time with her. For the first time, he began to understand her relational needs and messages. She became happier and felt closer to him because they started to communicate more.

Her radar picked up that the relationship was falling apart. The captain of the ship (her husband) thought this meant that he had to just work harder toward the goal of giving her more things. The radar was buzzing but making no sense. He heard the words, but misinterpreted them. When they really started talking to each other and understanding the relational messages, it simplified their lives.

A husband and wife are different from each other, but they can complement each other. The world needs radar and battleships that work together. There is infinite potential tied up in a couple. When you bring the God-reflected gifts of both together—they complement each other and have a greater capacity to make better decisions.

A husband and wife being together in communication and harmony is part of God's divine plan to reflect Himself to this world. Let's make every effort to figure out how to work together as a couple, despite our very different makeup.

Questions for Reflection
Chapter 4

1. As a couple when has your "battleship and radar" worked
   well together? How did you complement one another?

2. When has your "battleship and radar" not worked well
   together? What went wrong?

Notes

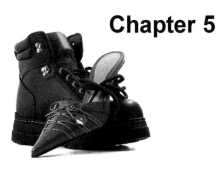

Chapter 5

Communicate Rather than Clash

M
en and women innately communicate differently, so it is no surprise when communication challenges arise between husband and wife. These obstacles of communication styles are in place even before we say a word.

Sometimes it seems like conflict is just at the surface ready to erupt. Then, all we have to do is make that one statement and it all blows up in our faces! We find ourselves asking, "Why is it that every time we talk it turns into an argument?"

Effective communication is not something a couple automatically knows how to do; they have to learn the skills. Communicating effectively in a relationship is a skill to practice in order for the relationship to move ahead in a healthy manner. It takes a great deal of effort, but it can be done.

In this chapter let us look at three things to learn about each other that will help us to communicate better. Learning how to recognize our spouse's *focus, purpose, and emotions* will go a long way in improving our communication skills.

Recognize your spouse's focus

When a woman and man communicate together, they have a differing focus. Guys are usually focused on goals and the long term picture. Women often communicate in the conversation relationally and focus on the short term aspects.

Let's say a couple is moving into a new house, but it is not move-in ready, so they have to live in an apartment for six months. In the apartment there is a huge picture window that needs draperies for privacy.

The husband says, "I have an old blanket that I used in college that is about the right size. We can tack it up and cover the window. We will only be here for six months." Suddenly he feels the tension rising in the room.

"I cannot believe you said that!" his wife says. "We are not hanging up an old blanket over the window for six months! How dare you even think about it!"

The other side of the coin is the woman's way of thinking. Her very different focus comes through like this: "Oh, this is such a lovely picture window. I can just imagine beautiful draperies accenting the room. For about a thousand dollars we could find just the right window treatment."

Now he is in disbelief. It is his turn to respond, "What are you thinking!"

The focus of the two is entirely different. Hopefully, somewhere in between the old college blanket and the thousand dollar window treatment, a compromise can be found!

Understanding his wife, the husband should look at the window and keep the thought about the "old college blanket" to himself. He could say something like, "Even though we are only going to be in this apartment for a short time, I do want to make it as comfortable as possible for you."

Understanding her husband, the wife should keep the thought about the "$1000 window treatments" to herself. She could say, "We need draperies for this window, but I want to work within our budget." Now this opens the door for more civil conversations in the future.

So, when you approach a "window," both husband and wife need to try to rethink their initial focus and first consider the other person. In that way, they can avoid those exchanges of, "How dare you even think that thought!"

Recognize your spouse's purpose

What is the real purpose of what you are doing in any given situation? When the wife is communicating a goal, she tends to focus on the *relational* aspect of achieving that goal.

A case in point happened one evening, while Linda and I were still separated and tensions were running high. Linda mentioned that we needed to purchase a new coat for our son, and she asked if I wanted to tag along. I was happy that she wanted to make any kind of connection, so I agreed.

We walked into the store. To the left was the shoe department. She walked into this department and soon we were looking at shoes. Before long, we walked into the next area which was the shirt department, and we started looking at shirts. Just past that department was the section displaying men's and boy's pants, and we spent time there.

I was starting to get fidgety. I thought to myself, *Maybe I misunderstood why we are here. I thought we were looking for a coat.* I really didn't understand why we were in the pants section. I had to ask, "Were we coming to the store to buy our son a coat?"

Linda said, "Yes."

I just couldn't help myself. I blurted out, "Then what are we doing in the pants department?" Immediately I wanted to pull those words back and stuff them into my mouth.

She gave me a look that could kill and said, "Okay then, we are not doing anything in the store; we are going home!"

So we left the store and it was a quiet ride home. Silence was a safe bet at the time.

Some time after that, she again invited me along to get something for one of our children. We walked into a store that had nothing to do with what we had come for, but this time I knew better than to say anything.

During the course of the evening, Linda tried on a pair of shoes and said to me, "These are pretty; I really like these. What do you think?"

Here is what I thought: *I know she has a pair just like those at home. I have seen shoes that look just like them. But I know that's not what I should say or this trip will end, and we'll be home in a heartbeat without getting what we came for.*

So, instead I just answered the question, "I think they are pretty."

She said, "Yes, they are pretty, but I believe I have a pair like them at home," and she put them back on the shelf.

Now how about that, I thought. I was still somewhat puzzled.

Soon she was holding up a dress. "What do you think?" she asked.

I said, "It's pretty."

She said, "Yes, it *is* pretty." Then she hung it back on the rack and walked off.

Not Right, Not Wrong, Just Different

Wow, I thought, *I can do this!*

We went through the whole evening like that with Linda showing me something and my commenting that it was *great* or *pretty* or *interesting!*

I had been trying everything and anything to have a healthy conversation and relationship with Linda and nothing worked. What finally dawned on me is that when we previously went shopping and she would have these exchanges with me, I was cutting them off by focusing on the task and not participating in the conversation.

I was so focused on the goal of getting what we came for; I was missing the very thing I was trying to do. Now I could see clearly an avenue for healthy conversation which would provide opportunity to restore the relationship with Linda.

It's hard to believe, but these days I initiate going to the mall and walking around. I just turn a "relational" switch "on" when I walk into a mall. I now understand that the relationship is the main purpose of those trips. If she looks at a ring that's worth ten thousand dollars, I take a deep breath and just answer the question, "That's pretty."

Needless to say, I'm secretly hoping she doesn't ask that second question, "May I buy it?" But I do not discuss that question until it is asked.

Recognize your spouse's emotions

There should be a Bible chapter and verse for this principle, a *Thus saith the Lord*, but I haven't found it yet! The principle is: *Facts do not penetrate emotion.* Guys really need to learn this!

Look at the diagram below. There are thunderclouds and lightening (signifying emotion) close to the woman. These emotions are integral to her. Observe that the arrow labeled "facts" drawn from the man toward the woman stops dead at the thunderclouds.

Thus saith the Lord:
Facts do not penetrate emotions.

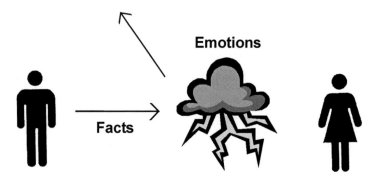

A man often tries to fix the situation with "facts" because that is what he knows to do. The facts go from his mouth, hit her emotions and ricochet off into the ozone.

In these cases, when a woman is in an emotional state and a man presents the facts, they rarely are able to reach the woman's mind for her to sort out and deal with them. They ricochet off the emotions and never penetrate. Let's say a husband is mowing the lawn and his wife drives up and stops in the driveway. She exits the car and is really upset and shaken. She exclaims, "Someone hit me when I stopped at the traffic light on the way home."

The husband quickly glances at the car and sees that not much damage has been done. There is a broken taillight and a small dent in the fender. In an effort to reassure his wife he

Not Right, Not Wrong, Just Different

says, "Well, we don't have to worry about it; we have insurance." His wife is not comforted at all. In fact, she seems a little angrier and repeats the details of the accident again.

The husband, thinking that maybe she didn't hear him the first time, says, "There's no need to be angry; we have insurance."

Now, not only is she angry; she is angry at her husband. She says, "You care more about the car than me!" and stalks off.

The husband, fed up with her responses, then says something like, "You're so irrational no one can talk to you!"

Does this sound familiar to anyone? What can we as men do? For one thing, we can recognize that *facts do not penetrate emotions*. If the husband could step back, he would realize he could do three things to help in that situation.

Recognize the emotion He should call his wife's emotion what it is—anger. "I can see you are angry." In saying that, she hears that he heard her. Now she feels they are on the same page.

Validate the person When he validates his wife he is saying that the feeling is legitimate. "I can see why that made you angry. I would have been angry, too." That says the husband understands.

Be available to the person "Is there anything I can do?" This communicates that the husband cares. He is making a connection. The wife feels he cares about what she has experienced.

Now the wife will more than likely say, "Well, it will be okay because we have insurance. They will take care of the car."

This whole incident is not about the insurance. Neither is it about the car. It is about her and what she is experiencing! A husband will always fix the car, but he will remain in trouble if he does not realize what the real issue is—his wife needs to feel loved, protected, and understood. In these types of situations, we as husbands need to stop leading with statements like, "We have insurance." She knows we have insurance!

This even applies to emotions related to happier circumstances. Suppose your wife's mother sends her an heirloom vase that has been in the family for years. She opens it up, and you state that it is the ugliest vase you ever saw! To her, this seems like a direct attack on her mother, even though you were just stating it was an ugly vase. A more proper first response would be, "Oh, isn't it nice of your mother to think of you?"

In light of that statement, your wife will probably say, "Yes, it's nice she thought of me, but this vase sure is ugly! We'll put it in the basement and when she comes to visit we will set it out!"

A husband must realize he does not have to have the factual answer to everything that comes up. The first, and most important, connection with his wife must be relational. After that he can discuss the factual things.

Now, certainly, I am not saying that guys are entirely unemotional or insensitive. The same can happen to them in an emotional situation because even with men "facts do not penetrate emotion."

In a marriage it is so important to understand this concept of how a woman and man are wired and how they usually make connections. By the way, God made us this way.

If we don't believe God has made us this way then we believe the other person is just wrong. When we determine the other person is wrong, we stop listening and start correcting that person. Ultimately, this ends up communicating that we do not like the person. To prevent this from happening, it can be as simple as learning how to recognize your spouse's *focus, purpose, and emotions* in a conversation.

Communicating relationally

After the first year that Linda and I were separated I knew I had to do something to help us to interact. At that point, she was not open to interacting at all. As far as she was concerned, our marriage was over and she was moving on. I worked during the day and she worked at night. I would come over and keep the children at night until she came home. This schedule enabled me to have consistent contact with Linda.

When our paths did cross, I tried to engage her in conversation. I wanted interaction, so I would ask her, "How are you doing?"

She'd respond, "Fine." I knew what that meant. She didn't want to talk to me. I persisted and occasionally could engage her in conversation. I learned to ask her questions about herself, and sometimes we would converse for awhile. Since our relationship was literally almost non-existent, if I ever disagreed with her, she was finished. Our conversation would end abruptly.

Wanting our conversations to continue, and not wanting to be dishonest when I disagreed with something she said, I discovered a phrase that became very helpful: "That's interesting," I would say. This phrase helped our conversations to continue in a much healthier way. Because of my previous insensitivities damaging our relationship, I now had to handle this fragile situation by paying much closer attention to what I said and how I responded to her.

One evening, Linda came home at 1 a.m., the normal time after her nighttime job. I saw something was wrong. "Is everything okay?" I asked. "It seems like something is bothering you. I'd really like to know what's going on. Do you mind telling me?"

Slowly, she started sharing. Very soon, she started pouring out her thoughts, emotions, and hurts.

Suddenly I knew I must really pay attention. I was getting everything at one time! She shared her heart, jumping from troubles at work to our relationship and how it affected her and back again to work.

I just listened. I didn't respond with a complete sentence the whole time. Basically, all I said was "Uh, huh. Really? Oh." I knew that if I was not totally attentive in this conversation, it might be a long time before she would talk to me again. I kept listening to her and never losing eye contact. Before I knew it, I looked at the clock. It was 5 a.m.!

She noticed the late hour. "Oh, you better go home. You have to go to work, and you need to get to sleep!" Then she walked me to the door and said one of the most amazing things I had ever heard, "Thank you for talking to me."

I immediately thought, *But I didn't say anything!* Yet here was another great lesson in relationships. I learned that just being there and listening amounted to "talking" to her! Although I said very little, I was very attentive. This action fell under the definition of communication—even talking!

It is true when they say that women talk almost three times as much as men, with the average woman chalking up

20,000 words in a day—13,000 more than the average man![1] When men are encouraged to talk to their wives, they often respond, "I don't know what to say" or "I don't have anything to say."

What husbands need to know is that they don't have to say much of anything. They just need to learn to pay very close attention to what is being said.

Consider this analogy of a woman and a pitcher full of water. A woman's emotions, after a long day, have filled up the pitcher. Many times the water is starting to slosh out over the top and the husband is trying to have a factual conversation with her. If the husband does not allow his wife to pour out her pitcher, the factual conversation will not go anywhere. What will happen is that she will drop the pitcher on his head if he is trying to have a factual conversation while her emotions are overflowing!

However, when a husband takes time to listen and allows his wife to pour out her pitcher, he then realizes he can have a factual interaction with very little emotion associated with it. Now he and she can be on the same page! Sometimes when Linda is sharing with me, I actually picture in my mind this pitcher of water pouring out. I wait until the water is poured completely out before I comment. I will even ask a question to make sure the last drop is shaken out because I don't want any water (emotions) left in the picture when we start talking.

Most guys have no clue what is going on inside a woman. They don't realize how a woman thinks with so many streams and trails as she integrates everything together. Guys tend to have a firm sense of direction that helps them accomplish their goal while women have better peripheral vision that helps them to see what's happening around them or to spot an approaching danger.

Men's brains are programmed to accomplish a task, which explains their narrow range of vision, while women's brains are able to decipher a wider range of relational information. Men are able to sort out information and archive it while women tend to "rewind" the information over and over again. The only way for a woman to stop thinking of a problem is to talk it over.

When a woman shares her problems with a man, she often is not looking for solutions—she needs someone to listen to her. In fact many times when a husband listens to the problem the wife is sharing, at the end of the discussion he will find that the problem mysteriously disappears.

Often Linda helps me out in this area. She will say, "I need to share something with you, but I don't need you to fix it." I feel totally relieved, relaxed, and ready to listen.

Therefore, when God brings two people together with such different outlooks, it is quite amazing that they can interact at all. However, when a husband and wife strive to understand the other's differences, instead of thinking they are *wrong*, they begin to move together in unity and completeness that becomes more of a reflection of God in this world.

Questions for Reflection
Chapter 5

1. As a couple has there been a time when "facts did not penetrate emotions"? How could you have handled it differently?

2. When has "listening" without any other immediate action gone a long way toward resolving a problem you were facing as a couple?

Notes

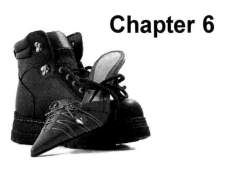

Chapter 6

Motivation to Save a Marriage

I grew up on a ranch in West Texas, and in a completely non-religious home. My mother and father were great, but they never discussed anything about God. We never went to church, and I knew nothing about Christ. In high school, some of my buddies were religious in a Christian ritualistic way. The only time I saw their faith intersect with their lives was when we were partying and drinking in the early morning hours and they would stop and attend a particular religious service. I waited in the car until they came back out and then we would continue on our way to finish drinking. Experiences like these and my lack of background made me think that religion was strange.

As I mentioned before, Linda and I got married at an early age. Both of us worked to put me through college. While I was in college our son was born. After college, I went to work for a man I knew in Yucca Valley, California, near the world's largest Marine Base.

During this time, I worked as a horse trainer. I ended up in a very bad financial situation and became indebted to my employer. We had a young family, had absolutely no money and neither of our parents had the money to bail us out. We were stuck, and I felt helpless and boxed-in.

One day I walked down a dried out sandy riverbed behind our house. With no place to turn and no place to look but up, I asked God for help. I fell down on my knees in the dry, sandy riverbed and started to cry out, "God, you've got to help me. This is just not fair." I was literally living in the desert and this was surely a desert experience!

The next day, I got a call about a new job possibility. After a short interview, I had a job at an accounting firm in San Bernardino, California. Within two weeks, we had a car, an apartment, and I bought two sports coats, two sets of pants and two shirts for the new job. I remember lying in bed during the first night in our new apartment, thinking, "What happened?" Just two weeks earlier, it seemed there was no way to escape the situation I was in, and now things had changed drastically. My thoughts turned to when I had prayed and asked God to help me. I became quite sure He had answered. It was a whole new concept to me. If I could pray and God would answer, then I wanted to know about God!

I decided to go to the library to find out about God. It didn't even cross my mind that you went to church to find God. In the San Bernardino library, I started my search. I guess I was going to look under "G" for God! In my search, I came across a book about the archeological history of the Jewish and Christian faith. I thought it could help so I checked the book out of the library. It was a very large book, and the library card revealed that no one had ever checked it out!

It turned out to be an excellent book. I read the whole thing from cover to cover. It described archeological finds and then referenced corresponding accounts in the Bible. After finishing the book, I thought, *I really should read the Bible so I can understand and discover who God is.* So I asked Linda if she happened to have a Bible. She thought she did and proceeded to pull out a box with old high school letter-sweaters and yearbooks. Sure enough, there was a red Bible in the box that Linda had received sometime during her teenage years.

I started reading the Bible at page one, just like any book. It took me about a year to finish it. I struggled through the "begats" and the food laws, but I was determined to find God. I had no history to unlearn, so I took everything at face value.

When I reached the New Testament, I read in Romans 3 that we all have sinned and fallen short of God's standard. "Well, that's me," I agreed.

As I continued on, I read that God gave Jesus as a *propitiation.* "They are justified freely by His grace through the redemption that is in Christ Jesus. God presented Him as a propitiation through faith in His blood, to demonstrate His righteousness..." (Romans 3:23-24).

What in the world was *propitiation?* I looked it up in the dictionary and it referred me to *expiation* and *atonement.* No one I had hung out with had ever used these kinds of words before! As I struggled with the definitions of these words and trying to insert them into the verses, the word "substitute" seemed to flash into my mind summarizing these definitions. The thought that stood out to me was that God gave Jesus as a substitute for me on the cross. I was forgiven. Something resonated in my spirit. I comprehended what God had done for me, and at that moment I was born again!

After I finished reading the Bible Linda gave me, I saw a paraphrased Bible in a grocery store. *I wonder if this one sounds any different from the one I read*, I thought to myself. So I bought it, and read the whole thing. I really liked it because it explained a lot of biblical questions I had. Now that I had read the Bible from cover to cover twice, I was starting to have quite a few conflicts inside.

Things were changing inside of me. I started to think differently. I proceeded to clean up my language because I didn't want to use certain words anymore. I still had all sorts of inconsistencies in my life. I threw away all the liquor from our liquor cabinet, but at parties, I would take a drink. Linda said to me, "Wait a minute, didn't you just dump hundreds of dollars worth of liquor away? Why are you drinking?" The truth is, I didn't know! All I knew was that before I was hell-bent on sin, but now my conscience bothered me.

One Easter, I decided we should go to church as a family. I had never been to church before. Which one should we go to? I looked around for a building with a steeple and that's where we went. For all practical purposes this was the very first church service I ever attended. On that Easter Sunday, the pastor told his congregation, "Look, I don't want you to get all hung up with the resurrection. It's not a big deal. It's really about how Christ lived His life."

I sat there, perplexed. *Yes, it is a big deal*, I thought. Why would the pastor say that? Surely he knows more about the Bible than I do, but I know that isn't right. After the service, he asked if he could visit our home. I declined. I was disappointed. It confirmed to me God was not in the church.

There was nothing I wanted there. They did not teach what I had been reading in the Bible.

At the time, I was the only Christian I knew. Linda had visited several churches as a child, but she was not a Christian. There were no Christians in my extended family or among my circle of friends or acquaintances. I didn't have any fellowship with believers, but I talked and prayed to God constantly.

I soon got a new job in Los Angeles, California, working for the federal government. Our daughter was born there. Then after three years, the government moved us to Virginia near Washington D.C. Many things were looking better, but our marriage continued to go downhill. I couldn't understand why our relationship wasn't working. All our interactions seemed to end up in intense arguments. In fact, I would often ask God, "Why can't you make Linda easier to get along with?"

When things finally fell apart between us, I got angry at God. *If You can't change her, who needs You?* I thought. I was mad at Linda; I was mad at God. As stated previously, I decide to pursue a worldly life-style. For a year, that is what I did.

One day as I was driving back home after doing something I should not have been doing, I said to God, *Well, God, did you see that? Did you see what I did? What are you going to do about it?*

Then I answered my own question, "You can't do one thing about it. Christ died for me, and I'm forgiven." I was like a two-year-old throwing a temper tantrum. Underneath it all, I knew I was forgiven. That was an unshakable reality to me. But I was kicking and screaming because I was hurt and frustrated. I thank God that He lovingly allowed me time to process through it. He kept His constant hand upon me.

After a year of foolish and sinful behavior, I had had enough. This was not the way I wanted to live. I was convicted that I really needed to work on my marriage. Of course, by now other than my connection with our children, Linda did not consider me to have any part in her life whatsoever.

One day, I simply made the statement to Linda that "before the Lord, I want to work at our marriage and try to make things better." Her reaction was predictable. She thought I was out of my mind to even think we had a marriage worth saving.

"You do whatever you want to," she responded. "There's nothing here."

With that rejection, I started to read through the scriptures again. "What should I do, God? My wife says she doesn't love me." I kept reading God's Word, and I must admit, I was looking for some kind of escape clause.

Husbands, love your wife as Christ loved the church

I read Ephesians 5:25-33 about the marriage relationship. Something jumped out at me. Four times in that section, it tells the husband to love his wife. But it didn't say anything about the wife needing to love the husband.

"Well, this stinks," I said, "God, why don't you tell the wife to love the husband? Linda says she doesn't love me, and it seems like You are saying, 'so what'! This doesn't make any sense to me!"

I decided to look up what *love* really meant. Everything I read described an *agape love*, an unselfish love, a sacrificial love. Then I read that a husband should love his wife like Christ loved the church. How did Christ love the church? Oh, that's right, He *died* for the church! And He died for us while we were still sinners!

I thought, *This sounds unbelievable, but if You say it, Lord, I'm going to do it! I don't really know how this works but I believe You, so if this thing falls apart, it's not going to be my fault.* Little did I know, this would be the best decision I would ever make in my entire life.

Linda wasn't being very cooperative. She knew which of my buttons to push to send me over the edge. But the good news was that it was almost impossible for her to make me mad. Okay, there were times! To be honest, there was a hole in my car's dashboard where I had punched it in anger after a frustrating time with Linda.

But most of the time, I was patient and kind. I decided to do what Jesus wanted me to do—to love my wife. If she ever needed anything, I would be there for her in a heartbeat. I really started to pay attention to our relationship. It didn't exactly make sense to me, but I was doing what the Bible told me to do.

Linda later told me that when I treated her so kindly and she was starting to warm up to me, she became afraid and tried to mask her feelings with sarcastic and negative comments. She didn't want to get hurt again. *Another lesson of life here; my focus had moved from Linda and her actions to Jesus and attempting to do what HE wanted.* Therefore, my actions did not fluctuate according to Linda's behavior.

It was a slow process, but by being obedient and continuing to love her unconditionally, healing started to take place in our marriage. We were becoming more and more cordial to one another, and some of the walls between us were coming down after a year and a half of attempting to love her like the Bible said.

One day, after Linda and I had gotten back together, I was reading the Scriptures, as was my custom, and came across 1 John 4:19: "We love because he first loved us"(NIV). I flipped back to Ephesians 5:25 where Paul spoke about husbands loving their wives like Christ loved the church and laid down His life for her. Now I could understand why the Scriptures didn't say anything about the wife loving back, it was just understood that it would happen.

Something clicked in my head. When Christ loves us and we understand that love, we can't help but love Him back. When a husband loves his wife like Christ loves us, she will eventually respond to that kind of love and can't help but love him back! It is a promise God gave. It is like a divine cause and effect, an eternal law! I didn't understand this when God told me through the Scriptures to love Linda when it seemed so hopeless, but I did because God said it. This is another lesson in life. Do it because God says to do it.

Because of our human nature, and living in a world that does not promote Christ's values, I understand that not all marriages work out. I thank God for His healing hand on those who have gone through broken relationships. However, Christian marriages should have a much greater success rate than they do. Both the husband and the wife have responsibility, but a husband has an unbelievable impact on a marriage relationship when he displays this kind of self-sacrificing love.

A wife can't help but respond to agape love

Because a woman is sensitive and relational, she tends to respond to this kind of love. She almost can't help but respond. A love dynamic starts unfolding in a supernatural way.

My motivation was to serve Christ and be obedient to Him. My motivation was not to get Linda back. Nonetheless, what happened was that Linda responded and the Lord started to restore our relationship, based on my being obedient to Him.

It is interesting to note that Linda had responded to my selfless love (which was really Christ's love), even though she had not yet determined to follow Christ. She was not yet a Christian. This is even more evidence of the tendency for a woman to respond to Christ-like love.

When Christ talks about us as His church, He says that He is the groom, and we are His bride. He loves us so much that He sacrificially laid down His life for His bride.

Because He loves His bride so much, she responds to Him. "For God loved the world so much that he gave his one and only Son, so that everyone who believes in him will not perish but have eternal life" (John 3:16). "We love because he first loved us" (1 John 4:19 NIV).

We read in 2 Corinthians 5:21, "For God made Christ, who never sinned, to be the offering for our sin, so that we could be made right with God through Christ." He did all this for us to have a relationship with Him.

The picture of that kind of love in this world is the love a husband should have for his wife. One of the ways God communicates to a lost world is through the unconditional love relationship of a husband and wife. The husband shows the self-sacrificial love of Christ, and the wife will demonstrate the response of the church. They build a union through that love. Supernatural power comes and flows through a couple because of that dynamic. It's a powerful witness to the world around us.

Other places in the Bible, we are told to love one another, which of course include husbands and wives. However, I believe in Ephesians 5:25, God is trying to make a point about the dynamics of a marriage relationship based on how a man and a woman are made.

Why is that so appealing to a woman? Because she is made to respond to this kind of unselfish love, with no strings attached. Just as man is an initiator, woman is a responder. When she receives love she will respond with love. If a husband begins to love his wife sacrificially, unconditionally, then she will experience the love of God through him. She will feel the blessing of knowing security, trust, and care. She will be able to let down her guard and open up her heart.

A husband needs to step up and love his wife unconditionally. When things get tough and he doesn't think he can go any further, he does it because the Lord has asked him to do it. I guarantee he will see the fruit of it based on God's promises.

Questions for Reflection
Chapter 6

1. Why is it important for a husband to show unconditional love to his wife?

2. Why would a wife respond to unconditional love?

Notes

Not Right, Not Wrong, Just Different

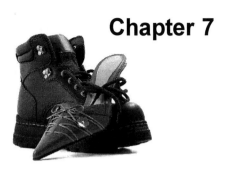

Chapter 7

Help Your Spouse Succeed

I believe there is infinite potential in a married couple. When you have two people, each with their own gifts and view of God coming together and complementing each other, even though they are so very different, we can see God's completeness and power being reflected through them. We can gain a perspective of who God is through viewing a healthy and Godly marriage. The couple begins to have a greater view of God and a greater view of the world, giving them a greater capacity to make decisions. The strength of couples is in their differences, not in their similarities!

As couples learn to appreciate the differences and work through them, trying to complement each other is the challenge. Remember, it's not right; it's not wrong; it's **just different!**

God has wired men and women so differently. We can become frustrated and annoyed and complain about the differences between men and women, or we can accept these differences and enter into the wonder of how God created us male and female. We can encourage each other's strengths and build upon what each has to offer.

Ladies, work with me on this, and please listen carefully. If a wife wants her husband to reach his full potential, then she needs to encourage him in the way God made him. How did God make him? God made him to *lead, protect, and provide*. He is motivated by those things and does well when he is achieving in those areas. Think about your relationship and what motivates your husband to reach his full capacity. If women can grasp this concept, it really is to their benefit.

Allow / Encourage the husband to lead

A wife should communicate to her husband that she needs him to take the leadership in their family. Most men will rise to the challenge. She should encourage him to go forward and take on the pressure of situations that are difficult for her. A simple example would be getting the car repaired. I don't know of one woman (maybe there are some) who is in her element when she has to go alone to a service station with all those male mechanics and deal with car repair issues. A good appeal to her husband would be: "Honey, that service man ignores me as a woman. I don't like interacting with him. I need your help and leadership in taking the car to the garage." A man tends to respond to that kind of appeal. He may complain, but he sees the need for his leadership. Therefore he will tend to step up and embrace the full capacity of the leadership role God intended.

On the other hand, if a wife does not allow her husband into that position of leadership, he will let *her* take that responsibility! That's one thing about men—they will be satisfied to have the wife take that role while they go fishing or play video games! He will turn over the responsibility to his wife, but in doing that, he will not reach the full capacity that God intended for him.

Allow / Encourage a husband to protect

A wife should always let her husband know that she needs his protection. There is something in a man that wants to step up and protect his wife. When there is a noise in the middle of the night, a wife should stress her need for him to go downstairs to check it out. He relishes protecting his family.

Imagine this scenario. After work, a wife meets her husband for dinner. They are both walking back to their respective cars across a darkened parking lot. A husband appreciates it when his wife asks for his "bodyguard protection" as he walks her to her car first before getting in his car.

Nevertheless, if she would say, "I'm not afraid, I can walk to my car myself," the husband will more than likely allow her to do so. A husband will take his wife's statement about not being afraid at face value and allow her to walk to her car alone if she wants. He has no problem with turning over that responsibility! Yet at the same time, the wife has denied the husband the opportunity to step up to his God given role as protector. As a result, the man will not think of himself as his wife's protector and will not reach his full capacity that God intended.

Allow / Encourage a husband to provide

A husband needs to be in a position where he feels a necessity to provide. If a husband has the sense that he must provide, he will step up and do it. After all, it is built into him to be the hunter and complete a successful mission. If the wife tells him he is not doing a good job providing and she can make more money, he will let her do it.

If a wife wants her husband to feel a necessity to provide, she must encourage him to do it. She should let him know how much he is appreciated and how important he is to her and the family. He will usually step up, because it is built into him to provide. In doing so, he reaches his full, God-intended capacity. A man is wired to do well in positions of leadership, protection, and provision. More importantly, a wife needs to understand these areas serve as a source of motivation for a man.

Let me give you an example that illustrates the point. If the propellers of an outboard motor on a fishing boat are outside the water while you crank it up and throttle it full force, it will just spin effortlessly, and very quickly burn up. However, if the propellers are down in the water and you throttle it full force, it will strain under the pressure, but run smoothly and last almost forever. The motor is made to be in the water, not out of it.

A man is like that outboard motor. He is made to be in the water, under pressure and having the responsibilities of leading, protecting and providing. Like that chug, chug of the motor in the water, the man may complain, but like the motor he will last forever. When his wife takes that responsibility from him, the husband becomes like a motor out of the water, just spinning under no pressure and never achieving the purpose for which it was designed.

From this illustration, you ladies have a great lesson; all you have to do to get an outboard motor back in the water is to lightly touch it with your hand and it falls back in. So, a wife's job is to cooperate with God and always encourage her husband back in the water of his responsibility, and he will motor on, and do it well!

Give men an opportunity to step up to the plate

We had a rule for our daughter Nicole, that whenever she was asked on a date, the boy had to come and ask me first for permission to take her out. Our son had the same rule. He had to ask the parents of the girl he was interested in. Of course, this really cut down on most casual, spontaneous dating in our teenagers lives!

Please understand I am not advocating "to date" or "not to date." My wife and I made a decision based on our situation and our children. We certainly honor those who look at this whole issue differently. However, I do want to share an insight we learned about boys that helps us understand a man's basic makeup.

Typically the scenario would unfold with a very nervous boy coming to talk to me. Compounding the fact that it was quite difficult for a seventeen-year-old boy to ask for permission to date, the boys also knew I was a pastor. The intimidation factor was high!

I would usually sit down with the boy and wait for him to start talking. Sometimes he would sit there for a while fidgeting, hoping I would initiate the conversation. I did not make it any easier for him. Finally, after a few gulps, the boy would manage a sentence, "Mr. Mitchell, I would like to take your daughter to [some approved function]."

Assuming our daughter had already told me she wanted to go, my response was short and straightforward. "Well, that is very nice of you to ask," I would respond. "But I want you to know that Nicole is God's gift to me, and I am responsible to God to protect her and take care of her. So when you take her someplace, I am delegating that authority to you and you are responsible to God for her."

Sometimes the expression on the boy's face was just comical because of the fear that streaked across it. I knew he was thinking, *Gosh, I just wanted to ask her to a school function. What am I doing? This is more responsibility than I bargained for!* I would give him no mercy. I would continue, "I want you to stay in public places, and *you* take her there and *you* bring her back."

Nicole revealed to me later that the boys who dated her were overly protective of her! Just my few words making them responsible caused them to make an effort to conduct themselves responsibly on the date. They would make every effort to protect Nicole. She shared about several times when a boy would foresee a potentially difficult situation and make sure they avoided it.

One time while visiting a museum in Washington D.C. a questionable individual was coming down the sidewalk and the young man Nicole was with immediately put his arm around her and escorted her to the other side of the street. Also the boys were usually very attentive. Sometimes she had to ask, but they willingly opened the car door for her, walked on the outside of the street nearer the curb, and held the chair for her in a restaurant.

Years later I was teaching this material to several couples as part of a pre-marriage counseling course. One of the young men in the course had gone to high school with Nicole. As I shared about the rule for dating Nicole, he exclaimed, "Everyone in school knew about that rule!"

What is the lesson? God made men to *lead, protect, and provide*. Men are wired to do well under pressure. They'll step up to the plate if it is expected of them. Sure, they may complain, but they'll do just fine. If a wife understands this about her husband, she can help him reach his full capacity. If she takes it away from him, he will never reach his full potential.

The dragon and the dove dance

A man is made to kill dragons! You rarely see a woman killing a dragon in a fairy tale. Why does the story of the knight killing the dragon and saving the princess ring true? Because it fits. Several years ago, the Marines had a recruiting commercial depicting a guy killing a dragon. They knew that young males would be enamored by the idea that they could be a hero, too. You give a guy a sword, and he *wants* to kill a dragon. It's built into him.

That is what I did by giving my daughter's boyfriend a "sword" of responsibility. He knew what to do with it—use it to protect my daughter. I didn't even have to tell him what to do with the sword. He knew. It's in him to know.

The problem is that the ladies need to understand that the men know what they are doing. Men just need to be given the opportunity, and they will slay the dragon. It's in their nature.

Previously, I shared an analogy of a battleship and radar to help us understand how a husband and wife work together and fill in the gaps the other is missing. While this is true, the man has the role to protector in the relationship. Now here is another analogy to help us understand how a man in his warrior capacity needs to fight battles and yet protect the woman's tenderness.

Imagine with me that a knight is trying to kill a dragon with a sword in his right hand, but in his left hand, he has a dove he is trying to protect. That dove symbolizes a woman. It's not in a woman's nature to fight the dragon; she has her husband to protect her. She is just there, being her relational and sensitive self, and her husband is protecting her. It's not that a woman *couldn't* kill the dragon—she doesn't *need* to kill the dragon. The man will kill the dragon because he needs to. It's in his nature. At the same time, he is allowing the woman to be whom God has created her to be—sensitive and relational.

Picture the husband shouting and grunting as he fights the dragon with his right hand while periodically turning and speaking softly to the dove, making sure she is safe and secure in his left hand. If he shouted and screamed at the dove in the same way he yelled at the dragon, the dove would struggle to get away. The knight has to learn how to fight the dragon, and then sheath his sword while gently talking to the dove.

The hard part for the male is not killing the dragon; it is talking kindly to the dove! He is not the best at displaying those sensitive emotions. And a woman must understand that a man does not suffer emotional damage from slaying the dragon. A wife can stroke her husband's hand and attempt to sympathize with his "bad" day of slaying a dragon, but he doesn't need it. He is not damaged by the fight, although he may complain! What he needs is appreciation for slaying the dragon and positive reinforcement to do it again the next day.

It's a difficult place for a man to be. He is made to kill dragons, but he must also learn to be relational and more sensitive to his wife. A husband is required to do two extremely different things. This is the way God wants it. A husband must learn to put down his sword when he comes home from work and concentrate on speaking kindly with the dove.

Working through the differences

A young couple came to me for advice. They lived on the East Coast in the same area where the wife had grown up. The husband worked for his father-in-law. An opportunity had recently opened up for a job in Colorado for the husband. As he shared with me about the job, it really sounded like a very good fit and wonderful opportunity, but I knew better than to give quick advice. I started by asking questions, especially of the wife because she would be the one moving away from the place she grew up and where most of her relatives and friends lived. She assured me that this job seemed like it would be a good move and "it would help our marriage." They left my office happy and believing this was the right decision to make. About two weeks before they were to move, I got a call from the wife who was hysterical. "I'm leaving my mother and dad, my sisters, my brothers, my friends—this is crazy."

"What does your husband say?" I wondered.

"He said we discussed this thoroughly. We made a decision to go, and this is no time to be changing our minds."

As we talked longer, it became clear that she still thought the job and the move was a good idea, but she was in turmoil about leaving her extended family and friends. When she was able to isolate what the pain was—that it was the agony of leaving her friends and family, she calmed down. I then talked to the husband and encouraged him to acknowledge her feelings rather than telling her to "just get over it." She was leaving the only home she knew. It was painful to think of not seeing her family on a regular basis.

I encouraged the husband to allow her to cry and grieve. I told him she needed to work through her feelings of leaving her family, and he must be supportive. "She will probably cry the whole way there and for two weeks after you arrive," I cautioned.

Six months after their move, the husband called to tell me that they both loved it in Colorado, and it had all worked out. He said, "Like you said, she cried the whole way here, but it wasn't just two weeks, it was four weeks until she stopped crying!" Nevertheless, by being supportive and acknowledging her feelings, rather than discounting her emotions, the husband was now able to give his wife the sympathy and support she needed to make the transition.

There's no "wrong or right" in how the wife felt or "wrong or right" in how the husband felt—it was **just different**! We might even say that after killing the dragon, the knight learned to speak kindly to the dove.

What if you don't fit the mold?

There is a particular type of couple that sometimes has a more difficult time than others fitting in with what I share— that men, in general, are more focused on goals and facts and are less sensitive and relational, and women, in general, are more relational and sensitive. Indeed, psychological test scores and theories bear this out, showing that the female brain is predominantly hard-wired for empathy and the male brain hard-wired for understanding and building systems. However some men and women are partially programmed to the behavior and way of thinking of the opposite gender.[1]

This means there are times you have a male who is more sensitive than most men, or a female who is not as relational and sensitive as most women. If a really sensitive guy marries a less sensitive woman, they may feel what I teach does not apply to them. Don't be so quick to discount it!

This story bears it out. One time I was conducting a pre-marital counseling session for a couple. The young man was easy going and very sensitive. You could tell him about a difficult situation or a sad story and his eyes would fill with tears.

The young lady was career-focused, thought in black and white terms and was a real decision-maker. Although very nice, she was not very sensitive or relational.

On the surface, everything I shared about marriage and the differences between men and women didn't seem to apply to them. I told them, "I'm not sure what to tell you, I don't have any other material! So you pick out what fits and as long as you are talking and communicating, it's okay with me!"

At the fifth session of marriage counseling, they walked in the room, and it seemed the room temperature dropped several degrees. Something was wrong. As we started the session, they began to talk to me, but they did not make eye contact with each other. During the session, I made the comment that I think the man in the workforce can more easily take the day-to-day grind and stress than the woman. I went on to explain that the grind does not damage him because as a male, he likes to slay dragons! I continued to comment that this same kind of stress affects a woman much more deeply. At that, the young lady burst out crying. She buried her face in her hands and started sobbing loudly.

Well, that was a bad example! I thought. *That sure didn't work. What in the world...?*

I looked at the boyfriend, and he looked like the cat that ate the canary.

"What just happened," I asked him. "What did I say?"

He revealed that on the way to counseling, his girlfriend was telling him about a very difficult situation she was going through at work. She was explaining how she was being treated and how it hurt her. "And I told her that I wasn't there, I don't know these people. There is nothing I can do, so there's no sense talking about it. And besides, we are going to counseling right now," said the boyfriend.

I just looked at him and was trying to process what he had just said. And then it dawned on me, *He is a man! He is just like the rest of us. He thinks totally like a man! Telling his girlfriend that he couldn't help her, and wondering why she was telling him about the situation, since he could not factually provide a solution, put him in the same category that most men are in when it comes to relationships between the sexes.* Then I looked at her, bawling her eyes out over his lack of sensitivity to her. I almost shouted "Hallelujah!" *She is female!* I thought. *This couple is just like all the rest of us.*

The maleness in me really came out—I had some facts and now I could write all this down as important information! This was a breakthrough in the class.

I did finally refocus on the relationship at hand. When things settled down, I encouraged the boyfriend to step up to the plate and protect and lead in their relationship. I counseled him that he needed to understand who his girlfriend is, and if he didn't make the effort, they would have a very difficult relationship and marriage.

I also gave some advice to the girlfriend. "You are a decision-maker and that's good. But inside, you are a female. Do not deny being a female or the sensitivity inside you. Yes, you will see things in black and white. That is great, but allow your boyfriend to take the forefront so you can develop those sensitivities within you."

I explained that before they knew all this information, they were getting married under false pretenses. He didn't know who she was, and she didn't know who he was. If they had continued in their ignorance, and approached their relationship in this role reversal kind of way, it would eventually become destructive to their marriage. Apparently, this couple took their pre-marital counseling to heart. They married and currently have six children!

Nix the nagging!

Relationally a wife needs to make the connection and understand how a husband thinks and what motivates him. Women need to realize that they accomplish nothing by nagging because they are approaching their husbands all wrong. Since nagging never accomplishes anything productive another approach is necessary. A wife should approach her husband by telling him that she appreciates him for all the things he does and then she should clearly identify the needs with his related responsibilities. This becomes a baseline by which the man can measure successes or accomplishments. It is similar to the princess identifying the dragon that is threatening her and then assisting the knight with his armor and polishing his sword. Therefore, all the things necessary for the man to identify the need and the measurement for success are identified. The next step for him is clear. When a wife wisely communicates in a similar way that she needs her husband to lead, protect and provide he snaps to attention and is ready to slay the dragon! That is how he is wired.

Likewise, a husband must recognize he shouldn't send his wife to fight the dragon. If he does, he will damage her. When he steps up and goes into the battle, he allows her to be who she's supposed to be and he is who he's suppose to be and this builds a healthy relationship. The husband needs to remember that the battles and the dragons may be small and appear in the mundane day-to-day events like emptying the trash, but the accumulated victories make a big difference over the course of one's married life.

Again, we come back to the conclusion that generally men have a pronounced need to fulfill their goals and understand the facts necessary for their endeavors, while women rank relationship and sensitivity higher on their priority list. However, these relationship dynamics between a man and a woman are not a science but an art.

Every couple needs to discover what works for them. I am sharing from my own experience and what I've learned. Please evaluate and talk about all this as a couple. Maybe something different works for you. As long as you're talking and making a connection, it doesn't matter if you come up with a slightly different conclusion.

Questions for Reflection
Chapter 7

1. When have you applied the lessons in the analogy of the "dragon and the dove"? If not, how can you apply them in the future?

2. If you don't seem to fit the mold, why is the information in these seven chapters still important?

Notes

Not Right, Not Wrong, Just Different

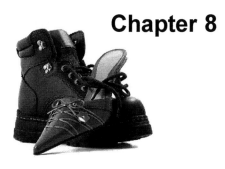

Chapter 8

Managing Marital Conflict

Most married couples know just how compli-cated married life is because of our differences as male and female. It's a challenge to understand each other and develop into the couple God wants us to be. If we are going to grow in oneness, we need to understand and even appreciate the differences between us. When we learn to embrace the differences rather than resist them, we will make progress!

Overcome the gridlock of "list keeping"

Every single person has whole lists of conflicts that have happened to him or her in the past. Not talking about them or pushing them aside will not make them go away. We remember conflicts, and often store them deep inside where we continue to add to the list.

When we keep a list of conflicts, a current conflict builds on past conflicts. A husband and wife may believe they are having a disagreement about one particular situation when in fact it is associated to a multitude of other situations that happened over the past several years. It's like a computer program that you have started with one click of your mouse, but it comes up with all the history as well.

Men, especially, think they are talking about one problem issue at hand, when they are really discussing not only that isolated issue but also the entire list of issues accumulated during their marriage relationship. Is this why they say a man never wins an argument?

Perhaps it is because a man doesn't understand all the issues that are involved. He just thinks about only one issue at a time—the current one. The woman will typically recall the past unresolved conflicts and almost never focuses solely on the current issue.

"Key word" arguments

I have seen couples in counseling get into an argument with each other, and I have no idea what they are talking about. I can't possibly follow because they are speaking in one-word codes.

They have learned over the years to argue with key words. They have only to speak one word, and it can bring up a whole history of past hurts. After years of unresolved conflicts a couple can become experts at this kind of arguing.

For example, I can sit down with a couple and start addressing an issue. Then as we are starting to make progress, one spouse may say, "Well, you remember the time we went to Georgia..."

"Georgia!" the other spouse explodes. "How about Disneyland, or Washington D.C.?"

Suddenly, they are both furious. One spouse continues, "Well, how about Jane?"

The other one sarcastically says, "Jane? What about Joe, or Ted or Nick?"

There are no complete sentences or thoughts in these arguments, only words that present pictures of past grievances. It is soon quite evident that they have never resolved any of these issues. Only one word is needed to place them firmly in the past conflict along with all the emotions they originally felt at the time in addition to the immediate issue at hand and all it entails.

One such situation came up years ago when I was a young pastor. The couple I was counseling was older than I, and they were batting words back and forth angrily. I was trying to help them resolve a difficult situation and help them better understand each other.

After a bit, I heard what I thought seemed to be the root problem. It sounded to me as if the woman had misunderstood her husband in a particular situation, and what had happened did not happen as she thought it did. I thought to myself, *Great, I can explain this to her, and she will be perfectly happy with my explanation and understand where she misunderstood her husband, and everyone will be so pleased with my wisdom.*

After I explained what I thought, the woman stared at me, and if looks could kill, I would be dead! I thought it was a pretty good answer, but her look told me I wasn't helping matters at all! Then, her comment absolutely floored me. "Well, that may be true, but he didn't come to little Johnny's christening."

What in the world did the subject they were talking about have anything to do with little Johnny? I thought. In fact, I knew Johnny, and he wasn't little anymore. In fact, he was 30 years old! They continued to argue and I sat there speechless.

In reflecting on the conversation, I realized first of all that I should not have been so quick to think I had the solution to the problem. I also realized that in this woman's religious background, having a child christened was a huge event, with extended family attending the large church celebration. When the husband refused to attend, it was both embarrassing and insulting to her.

A bitterness was allowed to grow for 30 years because the husband refused to attend the christening. Every argument they had from then on was built on that conflict because it had never been resolved.

Because she considered him to be wrong in not attending his son's christening, he could never again be right about anything. Therefore, thirty years later when I explained how the husband was probably correct, she jumped back to a situation that was on the tip of her tongue.

Keep short accounts

Couples must deal with problems when they come up. If they don't, all future troubles are built on the issues left unsettled. After a while, husbands and wives will have disagreements built on the cumulative effect of all the other disagreements they've had over all the years, and they will never be able to resolve anything. Now, that should scare married couples to death—scare them into finding a solution, that is!

What can you do? You must uncover those issues, deal with them and find forgiveness, then you can work with a clean slate and handle conflicts individually as they come up. When you begin to take steps to strengthen your relationship, it is imperative that you realize that the current issue is rarely the real issue. That is why many times we say to each other, "I don't understand; this is too complicated; you are unreasonable; what are you talking about?" There is always a reason. But it may be complicated by the very long lists we tend to keep.

Pay attention, have manners, will travel

Along with keeping short lists, we need to learn to practice developing positive lists. I heard of a poll that was taken which asked what women wanted most from a man and also what quality they wanted most from a man. The results concluded that what they wanted most from a man was for him to "pay attention to them." What quality they wanted most from him was for him to "have good manners."

Why would women want these two things? How do those two things connect? A woman realizes that when she walks to a door and a man opens it for her, it is because he knows she's at the door. He is paying attention.

At a party, a man says to a woman, "May I get you something to drink?" He pays attention and acknowledges that she is there. At the same time, he is displaying excellent manners. A man having good manners is a man paying attention.

Expectations

Another fascinating subject that ends up on our list is unfilled expectations. Expectations are what we normally expect! Most husbands and wives think of themselves as reasonable. So if the husband thinks he is reasonable and the wife thinks she is reasonable, then what the husband expects is reasonable and what the wife expects is also reasonable.

Right? Not really, because herein lies the problem—most husbands and wives don't bother telling their spouses what the expectations are, because *they think the other ought to know.* Why? Because it is expected.

One spouse may have the expectation that the other will share the cooking and meal cleanup or squeeze the toothpaste tube from the bottom. Then, when a spouse doesn't, the other one says, "See, he/she is inconsiderate because he didn't do what was expected. Any reasonable person would have done such and such!"

Let's say a wife has five different tasks she expects her husband to fulfill. These expectations are never directly communicated, but he is really paying attention and focused on his wife and therefore fulfills four of her expectations.

However, he does not do the fifth. She thinks, "If he had cared, he would have done what he was supposed to do—the fifth task." Since no credit is given for what we are supposed to do, the wife asks her husband why he didn't complete the fifth task. Incredulously he may immediately respond, "Look at the four tasks I did!"

How do you avoid this kind of thinking? Is the answer to not have any expectations? That's almost impossible to do. One of the things you can do is recognize when this scenario is taking place and identify and talk about expectations with one another. "I felt disappointed because such and such didn't happen." Together you can identify your expectations and then recognize what each person is thinking.

Husbands and wives need to be open to hear what is communicated. Then they can talk about what they perceive as normal expectations in the relationship.

Many times they become aware of what they need to talk about because their emotions will tell them. Those things inside that cause their heart to drop or make them irritated will tell them that they need to communicate and express how the situation really bothered them.

Workings of the mind

As if things are not complicated enough, men have the ability to compartmentalize things, while women's minds usually work fluidly with many different subjects interacting. You could say that a man gets his information from his desk in a completely different manner from a woman. A man's desk has all the information in different drawers. When he talks about a certain subject, he opens up one drawer, gets that information out and talks about it. When he is finished with that subject, he puts that information back, opens up another drawer, and pulls out other information and discusses it.

A woman has the same information, but all the information is on top of the desk! It covers the top completely and is interconnected. She jiggles the paper at the top left-hand corner of the desk and an eraser falls off the desk at the other end. It is all connected in some way. So when she talks, her mind works in this interconnected way. One subject is interconnected to many others.

So you can imagine that in a discussion between a man and a woman, the man pulls open his drawer, and takes out papers pertaining to one particular subject that he believes they are discussing. The conversation is started, and the woman seems to change the subject because she believes the subject at hand is linked to another issue.

The man says, "But that's not in this stack. That's not what we are talking about now." So the man takes the stack of stuff from the first subject matter, re-deposits it in the drawer, and opens up another drawer and pulls out a stack of papers pertaining to the second issue his wife brought up so he can talk about it.

A woman processes things all at once in a millisecond, while a man hasn't even gotten the desk drawer open on the other thoughts. Men and women must learn to understand how the other thinks so they can communicate more effectively.

A warning: Stay away from phrases like, "You are unreasonable. You are not listening," because this may not be true. It's better to say, "Explain how you got from there to here. I need to understand." One person has to take the time to explain, and the other needs time to process it.

You need to understand how the other person got from position A to B. *You don't have to agree with it, but you must take the time to understand.* Once you understand where the other person is coming from, you can have an informed discussion. It takes a lot of time and effort, but let's be candid—how long are you going to be married, or even better, how long do you want to stay married?

What do guys need to know?

If men can fully grasp the following concept, they don't have to read this book. That's why I am only sharing it here.

Here are three unique things you need to know about a woman. *She needs to feel cherished, remembered, and validated.* Notice I said she needs to "feel." I did not say she needs to be "told."

Women want to "feel cherished"

Men seem to have a problem getting their masculine arms around this word. At the same time women fully understand the meaning of the word *cherished*. A husband cannot just tell his wife she is cherished; she must feel it. He will know when he has succeeded because she will tell him when she feels cherished.

I could give you a definition from Webster's Dictionary, but that doesn't work because we are talking about *feeling cherished*. I think the best way to define *feeling cherished* is the following picture of a dad and his daughter.

Let's say his four-year-old daughter skips into the room with her fancy Easter dress on. "Hi, Daddy!" she says. As he looks at his little girl, his eyes light up with unconditional love.

Guys, this is it! Grab hold of it. What this man's heart communicates at this moment and the expression on his face screams forth to his little girl that she is cherished. He does not have to say a thing. She knows it by the expression on his face.

Believe me when I say a wife will know when she is cherished by her husband. This is a heart issue. Husbands, do your eyes light up with unconditional love when your wife walks into a room?

Women want to "feel remembered"

A woman wants to be remembered which communicates her husband cares. Hallmark will never go out of business because they understand this concept! It's important for a wife to know that her husband has remembered her birthday or their anniversary. That's why a man gives a woman a card or flowers—he is telling her he has *remembered*.

You rarely hear a guy say, "My wife forgot our anniversary!" But a woman will say it and be genuinely hurt if her husband forgets. She has a need to feel remembered. If she feels remembered, she will be much more secure in the relationship.

Women want to "feel validated or understood"

When a husband listens to his wife's feelings and tries to be more understanding, he is essentially giving her the validation she needs. Validation is saying, *"You are okay. I care for you. I understand where you are coming from. I can understand why you feel the way you do."*

Women are relational and sensitive and, as a result, feelings can be hurt and sensitivities can be damaged. So, when a husband validates his wife, he is communicating there is nothing wrong with her. Therefore, she is okay and it doesn't make that much of a difference what the rest of the world thinks. Their relationship grows stronger.

What do women need to know?

We do not want to let the ladies totally off the hook. Women need to remember that men think completely different than they do. Therefore, a wife needs to focus on what a man needs from her. *A husband needs to know he is admired and respected by his wife.*

Men want to "know they are admired"

A wife should let her husband know that she believes in

his talents and skills and is supportive of him. What really connects with a man is when his wife makes him feel like he is her man, and she is proud of him. A simple statement of "I'm proud to be your wife" speaks volumes to a man. It motivates him. When a wife says, "You're the man; kill the dragon for me," that's what he will do. A wife must show appreciation for her husband's role in the family. He is inspired by his wife's admiration.

Men want to "know they are respected"

Ladies, remember when I was talking about Ephesians 5:25-33? Remember in that section of Scripture, it tells the husband to love his wife four different times.

Also recall it didn't say anything about the wife loving the husband. However, it does say something specifically to wives. Because wives are made to be so sensitive and relational, God does not need to tell them four times like the husbands so He just says it once, "...the wife must *respect* her husband" (Ephesians 5:33).

Ladies, you need to grasp the magnitude of this statement. When a wife fails to show respect for her husband, his words or his decisions, she is destroying his confidence. When she is critical and disrespectful she undermines him at his weakest point. When a wife makes negative comments about her husband's thoughts and opinions, or gossips with her friends about her husband's idiosyncrasies, she is communicating that she does not respect him. Due to the way a man is wired, negative comments like these tear down his sense of personal worth and value, stunting his leadership development in the home.

A wife does well to give her husband opportunities to lead, provide and protect which show him respect. Giving him respect creates a safe environment in which he can carry out his duty to love his wife. When a wife grasps this concept of respect, it will be a huge breakthrough in her relationship with her husband.

Physical and sexual relationship

In the physical makeup of men and women, we are as different in our attitudes and our needs as we are in everything else we have talked about. In fact, everything we have talked about in this book should be applied to the husband and wife physical relationship. The physical and sexual relationship is a natural outflow of a healthy relationship. If I could give you a chapter and verse on the physical relationship between a man and a woman I would give you Philippians 2:3-4. "Do nothing out of selfish ambition or vain conceit, but in humility consider others better than yourselves. Each of you should look not only to your own interests, but also to the interests of others" (NIV).

Your physical relationship should start at this unselfish mindset. When there is good communication, a pleasing physical relationship the way God intended can be accomplished. Hopefully, the following will give you a place to start in your own communication with your spouse.

What did we learn so far about a man and how he sees the world? He sees goals—the final act.

How does a woman see the world? She is relational and sees the world in a network of connections and relationships—the process. Do you suppose some discussion is needed here?

A man is stimulated by sight. He's like a light bulb that can be flipped on in an instant. A woman is stimulated by touch. It takes longer. She's like a slow-cooker. Do you see an issue here?

For a man, the physical relationship is an isolated event. For a woman, the whole day leading up to the event is important. The wife remembers the argument they had in the morning, and she will not feel very amorous that evening if it has not been resolved. The husband has probably forgotten it and certainly does not see the connection with the moment at hand. To the wife, it has everything to do with what is going on at the moment.

In addition, there should be a lot of non-sexual touches between a husband and wife. Husbands and wives are made to have physical contact. Guys often have to make non-sexual touching a pre-determined thought! A wife knows very quickly if it isn't and will respond with, "Hey, not now, we don't have time for this." When this happens less physical contact takes place during the day which does not build a healthy, warm relationship.

If a couple does not have good communication about their sexual relationship, ultimately the consequence will be that they will not give themselves to each other physically which is a breach in the relationship. When there is a lack of understanding about our physical and sexual relationship, typically, the woman will feel used and the man will feel rejected. What God has intended to be wonderful and for our pleasure becomes a great frustration. Lack of understanding will turn into a downward spiral. Let me give you a bottom line: Communication!

Reflections concerning these eight chapters

In every marriage, there are a multitude of issues and highs and lows. No one is exempt. If you look at a couple across the street and think they are not having any problems, it's probably because they are not talking to you about it. To think you are the only couple going through bad times is destructive thinking because you will then tend not to tell anyone and hold the problems inward. This will never lead to resolving any of things you are struggling through.

Linda and I have learned to become transparent with each other in our marriage because we know it is destructive to a relationship not to talk about these things. We also openly share our struggles because this helps others realize that when difficult issues arise, there is nothing wrong with them as a couple. Then they are more likely to unashamedly seek counsel during those times. As long as you are talking and working on the issues, you are on the right track.

Sometimes it may feel as though you are rock climbing on a cliff and have only a toe-hold. Based on what is offered in this book, you have a toe-hold, but it is a solid toe-hold on granite. You are learning that the differences are not insurmountable. Yet, in order to have more maneuvering room, you need to chip away at that rock so you can have a plateau to walk around on. How does that happen? By talking and discussing the issues over with your spouse, you will develop a greater ability to build a good healthy marriage relationship. God divinely brought you together to build that kind of relationship—a relationship with infinite potential, a potential that you could not experience alone.

Questions for Reflection
Chapter 8

1. When has an accumulated "list" of events confused the current specific conversation that you were having as a couple? How did you resolve it?

2. Why would a husband showing his wife that she is "cherished" make a difference in a marriage?

3. Why would a wife showing her husband that he is "respected" make a difference in a marriage?

Notes

Not Right, Not Wrong, Just Different

Chapter 9

For Wives: What He Really Needs
Gaining Insight into Your Man

There are so many things our spouse does or says that baffle us. By now we have hopefully realized that it's not wrong or right; it's *just different!* Our church men's retreat is a case in point. Women would be horrified at the men's interaction at an all-male retreat. To begin with, there is minimal organization. There are no name tags or assigned rooms. Men just walk into a room and throw their bags on the first bed they see.

Our behavior while playing sports is often outrageous. I have witnessed men literally standing and beating their chests, like King Kong standing at the top of the Empire State Building, upon scoring a point in a volleyball game. Or they walk around flexing their muscles, exclaiming "Yes, yes!"

One time during a volleyball game, I dove to hit a ball, connected with it as it soared over the net, but lost my balance in doing so. I ran smack into a concrete wall and fell down. My head was bleeding, and the men were saying, "Yay, Wallace, good hit! Good job!"

They offered me no compassion. A little blood is expected, even admired. Men are supposed to dive for the ball and run into walls while playing sports.

Another time during a paint ball game, one of the wives who brought in our paint guns observed us throughout the game. Afterwards she said to me, "I can't believe how you spoke to each other. If anyone talked to me like that, I would be in tears!"

It was another example of how men approach situations with a strong desire to make decisions, take action and speak directly. They are motivated by conquest and success.

So far in this book, we have talked mostly about the husband's mantle to step up in his marriage—to be the man he is supposed to be, and love his wife like Christ loves the church. We said he would only reach his full capacity when he steps up to his responsibility as a husband to lead, protect, and provide.

When I share with a husband that the Bible says he must love his wife as Christ loved the church, the statement usually seems overwhelming to him. But I encourage him that through Christ's strength, he *can* do it! He is made to be a dragon-slayer who relishes the challenge. Now we want to look at the lady's responsibility in being a positive motivation to her husband in his endeavor.

Here's the motivation!

What I am about to share is for ladies only. I share it with women because I think it helps them to understand the male species a little bit better. This will explain how a wife can help sustain an excitement and passion in her husband. Therefore, the same is sustained in the marriage relationship.

Envision with me a picture of a beautiful sunset. When men step up and become who they are meant to be, you could say they are instrumental in creating this beautiful picture, like a glowing sunset. Upon closer inspection of this picture, however, you see that in the center of the setting sun there is a small hole like a missing puzzle piece. You can miss it, but it's there.

A man may be doing what he is supposed to be doing. The marriage picture may look perfect and beautiful, but when you look at him more closely, there is that tiny hole, and it is at the center of his heart. The total picture looks fine—he is doing what he's supposed to—working and providing for the family—but there is a hole in his heart that eats away at him. His wife probably does not know anything is wrong. Nevertheless, he is slowly dying as a man because this little hole, this fatal wound, if not recognized, will be lethal over the years.

A husband typically will not talk about this hole, maybe because he does not understand it. Even if he understood it, he would not tell his wife. Why? He probably believes she would not understand, or *even worse* she might laugh at him.

This concept is hard to put into words, so I asked the Lord for wisdom to explain this wound in a man. What is the missing puzzle piece in the picture? What is this hole in a man's heart? I feel that God gave me immediately a picture from my past; I had perfect recall of this incident.

The picture that instantly came to mind was from 40 years before, when I was 18 years old. I had just finished playing a football game at my high school. I was walking off the field, after a rainy, but victorious, game. I had scored two touchdowns, and all was right in the world. My helmet was hanging at my side; it was sloppy and muddy, yet guess who comes tip-toeing across the field to see me? That's right, my future wife, Linda. She runs up to me, hugs me, gives me a big kiss, and now she has mud on her face. With my helmet in one hand and holding her hand with the other, we continue walking off the field. The picture is perfect. The hole in my heart is filled in. Can you see it? This is it! This is the missing puzzle piece! This fills the lethal hole in the man's heart! The battle! The victory! The princess!

Proverbs 12:4 says, "A worthy wife is a crown for her husband, but a disgraceful woman is like cancer in his bones." A wife is a husband's crown. She joins him as his crown. That means he walks off the muddy football field, holding his helmet and holding his woman's hand, and the hole is filled and the picture complete.

From Camelot to Shrek, we see this story played out. From James Bond to Gladiator to Brave Heart, to the prince and princess in Sleeping Beauty, there is no surprise that men long to be brave knights. Women long to be lovely princesses.

Remember what I required of our daughter while dating boys in high school? What does a seventeen-year-old boy know? Nothing. He certainly doesn't know enough to take my daughter out. But when he comes to ask me for permission to take my daughter out, and I tell him, "You are responsible!" he steps up. He snaps to attention and takes care of the princess. I have just ordained him as a knight, and he will take care of the princess because that is how God made him.

If he is not ordained and called a knight, he will never take care of the princess. The world tries to convince men that they are not knights. The world says we do not need men to lead, protect, and provide. The world says we do not need warriors to rescue maidens. When men do not believe they are knights, they will neglect their family and at their worse, abuse them.

News flash to women!

Your husband wants to be a knight in shining armor. He wants to be romantic. "But you don't know my husband," you say. "He is not romantic, nor does he want to be."

May I suggest that *in his way* he wants to be romantic? When we look at the big picture and focus on the one thing that is missing from the picture, we see the hole really represents the man's masculinity; his heart of a warrior; the knight in shining armor. That's the piece that makes this picture whole.

Most women are initially attracted to their man by that piece—his masculinity. However, many times, once they are married, facing all the pressures of life, they do a lot by their actions to destroy the very piece that attracted them. In his book, *Wild at Heart*, John Eldredge says, "Women are often attracted to the wilder side of a man, but once having caught him they settle down to the task of domesticating him. Ironically, if he gives in he'll resent her for it, and she in turn will wonder where the passion has gone. Most marriages wind up there." [1]

I tell men to love their wives as Christ loved the church; I have no mercy on men. That's their obligation and job! But a woman's job is to help fill in that piece in the picture. I do not tell him he must be the knight in shining armor, but I do tell him he has a job to do. The woman is the one to say he is the knight in shining armor. She needs to make an effort to do things that do not diminish his masculinity.

For example, when a princess's knight comes riding home, it is detrimental to say to him, "What are you doing in that suit of armor—you look ridiculous. Get the horse off the lawn! Look at the mess you are making! Why are you 30 minutes late? Sheath your sword, you are going to hurt the kids!"

He will feel like his masculinity is stripped from him, and he will get back on his horse and ride off. He'll never be that shining knight again. Why? Because his wife didn't let him feel like that knight. He will never want to expose himself again at the chance his wife will humiliate him. Notice that I used the word "feel." A wife must make her husband *feel* like a knight.

I am never going to play another high school football game. My wife is never going to run across an ankle-deep muddy field to come to greet me. However, she communicates to me in ways that make me *feel* the same way. She makes me *feel* that I am her knight in shining armor, and it reaches my masculine soul.

How a wife allows her husband to express his masculinity

A wife's day to day communication with her husband affects the way he feels as a man. When a wife is critical of her husband, harping on his weaknesses and belittling him, she communicates in a way that makes him feel like less of a man. When she says, "That's a stupid idea" it doesn't just communicate that she thinks it was a bad idea, it communicates that she thinks he is inferior as a man.

I'm not talking about conflict. I personally believe healthy conflict is good. It is a sign that couples are working through difficult issues. I worry about couples who don't have conflicts. I have previously warned men in this book about their behavior when interacting with their wives. Here I want to warn the wives to be more aware of the things they say to their husbands. Many times men get angry or withdraw, not because of the conflict, but because the wife has made him feel less of a man.

A smart and sensitive woman will recognize that there is a hole in her husband's heart, and she will fill it in the way she communicates to him. If she expresses herself in a way that makes him feel like less of a man, she has accomplished nothing. But with wisdom, she can present herself and communicate in a way that acknowledges his masculinity.

A retired man helped our church negotiate with a building contractor and secure plans to build our building. The man's wife and I were present as he expertly negotiated one particular deal. Afterwards, his wife turned to me and said, "Did you see that? Wasn't he just wonderful? I just love to see him work. He does such a good job." I could almost see the husband's chest expand as he patted his wife on the back in appreciation.

What was she saying, really? She was saying to her husband, "You're the man!" She filled that hole in his heart. His chest expanded as he put his arm around his princess. This wife knew how to speak into his life and communicate that he was her knight in shining armor.

Another thing a wife can do to make her husband feel like a masculine knight is in the way she takes care of herself. How does she dress? If she is a stay-at-home mom, does she put on a little makeup to look better when he comes home, or does she look like she's been working in a lumber yard all day? I promise you this, when her husband goes to work, every lady he sees is well-maintained and groomed.

Granted, a wife cannot focus her attention and efforts solely on how she looks on the outside. She must focus on the beauty that is inside and that inner beauty will shine out. A wife should make a conscious effort to present herself as a princess. In doing so, she is healing that hole that makes her husband feel like the man she wants him to be. If a wife wants her husband to step up and lead, provide for, and protect her, she must make him believe that she will follow him anywhere.

Husbands lead

Most wives want their husbands to take the lead. A woman longs for a champion or leader who will fight for her. Some may think, "But my husband has a lot of hurts in his life and needs a lot of help before I would follow his lead anywhere!"

If, in good faith, you can't tell him you'd follow him anywhere, you *can* say something like, "I can see God working in you. I appreciate who you are and how God has given you gifts to use. Let's explore your idea, and pray about it. I appreciate what you are doing for us." You fill the hole in his heart with this type of affirmation.

If a man loses his job, or can't provide, I promise you he feels worse than his wife does. If the wife tells him he can't provide, or that she doesn't trust him to provide, he will be destroyed. He may not show it. He may just go play video games or something similar. But he will not step up and be who he is supposed to be. He will feel emasculated.

Instead, a sensitive wife will recognize the hole and fill it. If her husband loses his job, she will make every effort to make him feel like he can make it. She will tell him that he has talents and abilities even if his boss didn't recognize them. God has equipped and made him special, and together she and he will make it!

Husbands protect

A husband wants his wife to feel safe with him. He wants to be her knight. One time, I made a man cry by explaining that his wife was his princess and he was responsible for her. He cried because it rang true. When a wife communicates to her husband that she is his princess, it rings true. If he is assured that his wife is his princess and he is responsible for her, his motivation is to step up and be "the man."

As we put this into perspective, we realize that guys really are tough. They can handle a lot. However, even though the hole we are talking about is a small hole, it is a hole in the heart. Therefore, it is lethal. Any hole, even a pin-size one, in the heart is serious. This is why it is so critical to a man's well-being to have this hole filled. If a wife communicates to her husband that he is her knight, she will help make the picture perfect. When you think about it——maybe it is the ladies who should cry when they recognize the hole in men's hearts!

When a wife walks in unity with her husband and communicates with him, he will be the knight he is supposed to be. Can you imagine what would happen in the fairy tale if the princess in the tower shouted down to the knight, telling him exactly how she wanted to be rescued? She proceeds to tell him when she wants him to start climbing the tower, what security equipment he should carry with him and where to place each foot. She meticulously describes how everything should go the way she imagines it so it can be a perfect rescue in her eyes. That is not allowing a husband to be the knight. It is dictating what she thinks are his knightly duties. A wife must let her husband be a knight as he sees it and is uniquely designed for.

She must discover what makes her husband feel alive and adventurous. Maybe some women are thinking they don't want their husbands to feel that way! But that is what most men want to feel. They have a craving to be challenged, grow and become all they are capable of. Take, for instance, three guys on our leadership team who are very different, but all very masculine in the way they think.

Paul loves to spend time in the mountains and hunt, so his wife gives him opportunities to carry out his love of hunting. She knows it is a way to release his masculine soul. For him, it fills the hole in the heart; it is the way he is wired. Christmas and birthdays are a cinch for his wife. She knows she can make him happy by buying him a camouflage outfit or a compass or a hunting knife.

Greg loves motorcycles. There is something about sitting atop a large motorcycle with its loud noise that makes him feel masculine. Is it romantic? Maybe. Greg proposed to his wife from his motorcycle! What does Greg need to fill the hole? He needs time to ride on the open road. It is an expression of his masculine soul that fills the hole in his heart.

Craig loves music. I don't think he likes to hunt animals or ride motorcycles. Playing music is a masculine expression for him. His wife knows that purchasing a new guitar or giving him time to have music lessons releases him into his masculinity. It fills that hole.

It could be golf, weight-training, running, the list goes on. A wife has to find out what it is that makes the picture complete, and then give him that outlet, or he will shut down. He will continue to go through the motions, because he is too tough to quit, but *he will lose his passion.*

This is not just about recreation. We are talking about touching the hole in his heart so he can be the warrior he wants to be.

I can hear some wives saying, "But, we've got a million things to do and he wants to go out shooting deer. We've got work around the house and he wants to take a ride on his motorcycle or practice his guitar." How a man is wired often becomes a frustration to a woman, but I have a feeling, though, that this macho stuff was what attracted her to him in the first place. It just becomes a tremendous inconvenience after they get married to carry it out! "Why don't you grow up?" is an oft used phrase a wife may say to her husband. "Now you have a family and important things to do."

Remember, a man doesn't think like a woman. The Bible proves it. It gives us action and adventure stuff like these verses:

> "The Lord will march forth like a mighty hero; he will come out like a warrior, full of fury. He will shout his battle cry and crush all his enemies" (Isaiah 42:13).

"Praise the Lord, who is my rock. He trains my
hands for war and gives my fingers skill for
battle" (Psalm 44:1).

And all God's men said, "Amen!"

Okay, ladies, here's the punch line!

Please listen closely and take this to heart. Remember the
scene I described of me walking off the football field? A very
important part of that scene was that *I was not alone.* I was
holding hands with Linda. Yes, a wife is the integral part of
the picture! The piece that fills the heart of a husband is not
just the *event*, it is the *princess* that actively makes him feel like a
knight.

It's the piece he cannot fill on his own. Only his woman
can fill that hole. God made it that way.

Now you have the desires of a man's heart and a
woman's heart fitting together—wives and husbands hand in
hand, walking together as they discover who they are. *For a
husband to be a true knight, he has to have a princess.* He must have
someone to fight for. That's the wife's role. *She inspires him to
be a hero. On a human level, she fills the hole in his heart.*

As I wrap up this book, I would like to leave you with a
few closing comments. The greatest relationship we will ever
have is our relationship with the Lord Jesus Christ. Knowing
that He died in our place for our sins on the cross and that by
trusting in Him, we are forgiven and have an eternal home in
heaven.

The second greatest relationship is the marriage relationship. I can honestly say that other than our relationship with
Christ, nothing on earth is more powerful and has more
potential than the marriage relationship.

My heart is to see the power of God flow out of healthy marriages. I believe God has given Linda and me that ministry. We want to see couples be everything God wants them to be.

God created man and woman exactly the way He wanted them. He designed the infinite potential in a marriage relationship. The differences we each possess combine to reflect the fullness of God Himself. When we complement each other we express a Christ likeness that is no less than supernatural. This is exactly what God intended.

Dear heavenly Father, I thank you for the way you have made us. You have made us to work together through the supernatural power of the Holy Spirit. We give you thanks in the name of the Lord Jesus.

Questions for Reflection
Chapter 9

1. Men, what makes you feel masculine, alive and adventurous?

2. Women, what can you do to let him feel masculine, alive, and adventurous?

3. After reading this book, can you rejoice in the way God has made us and say, "It is good!"

Notes

End Notes

Chapter 2

[1] "Understanding the Differences Between Men and Women," Michael G. Conner, Psy.D, Clinical & Medical Psychologist, www.oregoncounseling.org

[2] "A great marriage is not when the 'perfect couple' comes together. It is when an imperfect couple learns to enjoy their differences."
—Dave Meurer

Chapter 3

[1] Dr. Daniel Laby, Dr. David Kirschen & Tony Abbatine, "A Visual Profile of Major League Hitters," http://www.frozenropes.com/core/newsletter_details.asp?ArticleID=76, accessed January 2009.

[2] **Intuition** is the apparent ability to acquire knowledge without inference or the use of reason. It is "the immediate apprehension of an object by the mind without the intervention of any reasoning process" (Oxford English Dictionary). Intuition provides us with beliefs which we cannot necessarily justify. For this reason, it has been the subject of study in psychology, as well as a topic of interest in the supernatural. Psychologist Matthew Lieberman published a paper in 2000, entitled "Intuition: a social cognitive neuroscience approach," and discussed a possible biological basis for female intuition:

A review on intuition would be incomplete without reference to women's intuition, the colloquial notion that women have a sixth sense or a more able intuition faculty than men. Like intuition itself, women's intuition is often shrugged off as an urban myth. There is strong and consistent evidence that women are better encoders and decoders of nonverbal communication (Hall, 1984), and this evidence has frequently been cited as possible evidence of women's intuition (Graham & Ickes, 1997). Additionally, the hormone estrogen, present in greater quantities in women than men, directly affects the amount of DA [dopamine] released into the striatum (Becker, 1990; McDermott, Liu, & Dluzen, 1994; Mermelstein & Becker, 1995; Van Hartesveldt & Joyce, 1986).

Chapter 5

[1] Fiona Macrae, "Women talk three times as much as men, says study," http://www.dailymail.co.uk/femail/article-419040/Women-talk-times-men-says-study.html, accessed November 12, 2008.

Chapter 7

[1] "They just can't help it," Simon Baron-Cohen, The Guardian, Thursday 17, April 2003, http://www.guardian.co.uk/education, accessed January 2009.

Chapter 9

[1] John Eldredge, *Wild at Heart*, (Nashville, TN: Thomas Nelson, Inc., 2001), p. 82

Not Right, Not Wrong, Just Different

Contact Information

Wallace Mitchell III, Senior Pastor
Broadlands Community Church
21112 Stonecrop Place
Ashburn, VA 20147
703.724.0361 (church)
703.819.3202 (cell)

www.broadlandscommunitychurch.com
wallacebcc@aol.com

Not Right, Not Wrong, Just Different